TRADITIONAL
Knitted Lace
Shawls

MARTHA WATERMAN

INTERWEAVE PRESS

Cover design: Susan Wasinger, Signorella Graphic Arts
Photography: Joe Coca, Martha Waterman, and Lea Babcock
Technical editing: Dorothy T. Ratigan
Illustration: Susan Strawn-Bailey, Martha Waterman, and Lydia Kulesov

Interweave Press LLC
201 East Fourth Street
Loveland, Colorado 80537 USA
interweavebooks.com

Printed in the United States of America by United Graphics

Library of Congress Cataloging-in-Publication Data

Waterman, Martha.
     Traditional knitted lace shawls/by Martha Waterman.—Rev. ed.
          p.   cm.
     Includes bibliographical references and index.
     ISBN 13: 978-1–883010–48–5
     ISBN 10: 1–883010–48–9
     1. Shawls. 2. Knitted lace—Patterns. 3. Knitting—Patterns.
     I. Waterman, Martha. Traditional knitted & lace shawls. II. Title.
TT825.W377 1998
746.2'260432—dc21   97–53192
                                                                          CIP

15 14 13 12 11 10 9 8 7

CONTENTS

ACKNOWLEDGEMENTS

I would like to thank most sincerely:

Arlene Waterman, my mother, for the family history of shawls, books from the "old countries", and encouragement.

Sarah Johnson, for the books and catalogs she so generously sent me, and for her enduring friendship.

Betty Burford, who was so generous with her beautiful wool.

Julie Huffman-klinkowitz who lent a hand many times.

Franke Harte, who set me straight upon the path of tradition, *an sean-nos*.

Dianne Phelps, for her patient help.

Mary Logan Sweet, who sent me valuable information.

Eleanore Mast, whose work ranks with past masters, and who provides me with inspiration.

And *Tasha Tudor* for her appreciation of the first edition and her friendship.

Special thanks

to Anthony Montoya of the Paul Strand Foundation for use of the photo of Kate Steele
to Chris Bunyan and Mary Smith for the use of archival photos published in *A Shetland Knitter*'s Notebook
to Meg Swansen of Schoolhouse Press for her enthusiasm and encouragement
and to Diane and Ron at Shutterbug for their patience and diligence.

INTRODUCTION

There is nothing else knitted that I like to dream up, plan, knit, finish, wear, use, or give as a gift so much as a shawl. To me there is an endless fascination in the various shapes, stitch patterns, colors, and fabrics that make shawls my favorite knitting. As much as I love a good sweater, the fun of them is sometimes clouded by anxiety about fit, and besides that, they're finished much too soon. Sometimes the heavier weights of yarn make my hands ache, too.

But shawls are of lovely, light-weight yarn, their patterns are fun to knit (especially with a lot of yarn-overs), and they can be any size; they don't have to fit.

Shawls have enjoyed a central place in women's wardrobes many times in fashion history—in the Napoleonic era, in Victorian times, and then again briefly in the late 1960s/early 1970s during the craze for "granny" and "peasant" looks. Recently, paisley print shawls have made a comeback as a bright accessory over conservative winter coats and blazers.

Even when out of fashion, shawls have remained a staple clothing item among women who cared little for fashion's dictates: country-women and elderly women. Attracted by their warmth, usefulness, and practicality, these wise women kept a shawl on a nail by the back door, or over the back of their favorite chair. I know my Irish/Welsh great-grandmother did this; we have her shawl to this day (although it is a woven one). My mother recalls that Great-Grandma snatched up her shawl on the way to the henhouse, throwing most of it over herself and using a spare corner in which to collect the eggs.

The beauty of shawl wearing is in its flexibility. A shawl can cover any chilly part of your body—head, feet, knees, shoulders. Wool in particular holds in body heat. We know that simply covering the head and shoulders makes one feel instantly warmer. A shawl can do this quickly and easily, while a sweater leaves your head bare. When you're warm enough, it takes only a second to throw off a shawl. In a suitcase, a shawl takes up no more room than a sweater, but on a plane, or in the car, which would you rather take a nap under?

A shawl can also serve as a pillow, picnic cloth, umbrella (of sorts), carrying bag, or seat cushion. In a pinch, a shawl can be mosquito netting, an evening wrap, and a dressing gown (even a dressing room) all on the same trip!

If knitted shawls are a pleasure to wear and use, they are equally rewarding as a showcase for your knitting skills. Stitch patterns, yarns, and colors can range from the simple and charming to the very elaborate and elegant. Few who value quality handcrafts can resist the beauties of a well-knitted shawl. If praise and admiration please you, you can expect your fair share as a shawl knitter.

A handknit shawl also makes a splendid gift. A new baby and its mother, a child in the hospital, a friend moving away, even a bachelor brother-in-law can find warmth and comfort in such a gift, especially if made to suit the taste of each recipient. Such shawls may be treasured as heirlooms, providing a sense of continuity and security that no machine-made object can match.

All this in a simple knitted shawl?

Try one now, and see for yourself.

TRADITIONAL KNITTED SHAWLS

ORIGINS OF KNITTING

Knitting is a very ancient skill, but arguments about its origin are never-ending among knitting historians. Arabia is one oft-cited birthplace of knitting, Egypt is another. Richard Rutt, in his book *A History of Hand Knitting,* puts forth Syria as a possibility, but believes we will probably never know the truth about knitting's origins. Many early examples of "knitting" unearthed in archaeological digs, some dated as early as 256 A.D., are now known to be a kind of needle-made fabric from a technique called "nålbinding". The technique is still used in Scandinavian countries. But it's not knitting.

It might be reasonable to assume that knitting was first done by nomadic herders of sheep, goats, and camels who spun the fiber but did not stay put long enough to weave it. In *Cut My Cote,* Dorothy Burnham hypothesizes that woven garments were based on even earlier skin garments, so it may be that knitting evolved from weaving concepts. Given spun wool, a few sticks, and the need to keep occupied during constant travel, it could be that knitting emerged spontaneously. Possibly the first knitted shawl was rectangular or square, in imitation of woven fabric.

According to Rutt, the earliest surviving truly knitted pieces are a medieval Swiss purse and medieval cushion covers from a royal Spanish tomb. Most extant ancient knitting is opulent and costly, so we must assume that everyday knitted objects or garments do not survive because they wore out or were not deemed worthy of preservation.

Because so much of costume history has focused on upper-class fashions, the humbler knitting of the past remains largely undocumented. However, there is evidence that caps, stockings, shirts, and gloves have been hand knitted (by both genders, Rutt says) since the fourteenth century. William Lee's knitting

Kate Steele, South Uist Hebrides, 1954. © 1962. Aperture Foundation, Inc. Paul Strand Archive. Kate's garter-stitch hap shawl has a a wide band of Old Shale patterning.

machine, unveiled in the late sixteenth century, by no means put an end to handknitting. The mass production of steel knitting needles at about the same time probably had a greater impact on knitting because knitting tools became widely available. Circular knitting on many double-pointed needles was more the norm in early days than circular knitting is today, in spite of our technological advances in needle construction which have produced circular needles.

HISTORY OF SHAWLS

The first British "shawls" were the woven cashmere imports that arrived in the mid-eighteenth century. The word "shawl" is of Persian origin, and the imports were embroidered or printed textiles from Persia, India, and Kashmir. Fichus and shawls became especially popular following the import and use of sheer cotton muslin for "empire" gowns; the fabric was so light and the undergarments so insubstantial that extra warmth was essential. The imported wool tapestry Kashmir (cashmere) shawls later made so fashionable by Empress Josephine were imitated by weavers in Britain as early as 1780, according to Valerie Reilly in her book *The Paisley Pattern*. Knitting historian Lizbeth Upitis says the young Queen Victoria loaned her Kashmir and Persian shawls to the weavers of Paisley, near Glasgow, who learned to make woven copies of such beauty that the Queen purchased seventeen in 1842. According to her letters and journal, she wore one to the christening of the Prince of Wales.

Shetland lace shawls

It is very possible that the famous Shetland lace knitted shawls and stoles were, at least in part, imita-

Lace headsquare from the Shetland Islands. Courtesy of Chris Bunyan and Mary Smith, A Shetland Knitter's Notebook.

tions of the Kashmir and Paisley shawls. The famous "paisley" shape, which both Matthew Blair, an early writer on Paisley, and Valerie Reilly call the "pine" pattern, can be clearly seen around the edge of an Unst-made knitted lace shawl in the Museum of Antiquities in Edinburgh. The fern pattern seen on many lace shawls may be a version of the Indian date-palm pattern, or a tree entwined with some vine.

The overall configurations of the Kashmir, Paisley, and Shetland lace stole or square shawl are very similar: large centers of plain or allover design with wide, elaborately patterned borders. The rectangular Paisley shawls (or stoles) are probably also the inspiration for stoles made by the lace knitters of Scotland. In his *Guide to Paisley Shawls*, Frank Ames's diagram of stoles from what he calls the Sikh period (1819–1846) shows a marked similarity to the diagram that Sarah Don provides for traditional knitted Shetland lace stoles in *The Art of Shetland Lace* .

The actual origin of the Shetland lace shawl is as veiled in the mists of time as the origin of knitting itself. Families from the Shetland mainland and Unst have claimed to be the originators of the world's finest lace knitting. Knitting historians Sheila McGregor, James Norbury, and Alice Starmore all believe that Unst may have the best claim as birthplace of Shetland lace knitting. The Hunter family on Unst is certainly part of the legends; one of the Mrs. Hunters has a lace stitch named after her (page 36), in much the same way that Scots and Irish jigs and reels are named after their originators.

McGregor and Starmore agree that an Oxford merchant, Edward Standen, played a notable part in marketing and popularizing Shetland lace knitting, but it seems fairly certain that lace knitting was already established in the Shetland Islands before his first trip there in 1838 or 1839. However, knitted white lace of the sort used in stocking knitting was certainly made in Scotland as early as 1818. McGregor has discovered a lace sampler in the Kelvingrove Museum, Glasgow, with the date 1818 and maker's initials knitted in.

Norbury and McGregor both suggest that the women of Shetland began knitting lace in the early part of the nineteenth century after having seen European bobbin and needle laces brought in by visitors. Crochet lace also seems to have emerged at about this time—the 1830s or 40s—once again as an imitation of earlier laces. At the same time, the Paisley shawl was making its way to the far reaches of the British empire.

Haps or everyday shawls

Between about 1840 and 1870, which Blair cites as the end of the Paisley shawl's popularity, the knitted shawl, with some openwork, was made and worn for almost all occasions by all classes of women in Britain, Ireland, and North America. Among the Celtic and British people, the everyday knitted shawl came to be called a hap. The word is an antiquated one of unknown origin, according to the Oxford English Dictionary. It means "to cover up" or "to wrap up for warmth, as with extra clothing or bedclothes." A "hap-warm" was a warm wrap or cloak, while a "hap-harlet" was a coarse blanket used to cover a straw sleeping pallet. Eventually hap came to mean any type of everyday cover, from a shawl to a carriage rug.

The shawls called haps were almost invariably of a dark color or black to permit more wear with less washing, of a little heavier yarn than a fancier openwork shawl. Hap scarves or stoles were rather sturdily made in the same colors as shawls with color bands. They had an interesting zigzag appearance, and scalloped ends.

In her book on Texas pioneer women's clothing, Betty Mills extols the everyday shawl as one of the mainstays of the American pioneer woman's wardrobe.

During the Victorian era in North America, the shawl was knitted and crocheted in many styles and patterns; boas, fascinators, comforters, pelerines, tippets, capes, hoods, and mantles were all forms of the basic, everyday shawl, and as such, were shown in all the popular ladies' magazines of the time.

In *No Idle Hands*, Anne MacDonald notes the publication of knitted shawl patterns in the mid-1840s. Many women emigrating from the British Isles brought their traditional wools, needles, knitting sheaths, and pattern samplers with them to North America, knitting and spreading their handiwork as their families searched for new homes.

Shetland shawls

Eventually, a Shetland shawl came to mean any shawl made of Shetland wool, the light, two-ply yarn from native Shetland sheep. Later, "Shetland wool" became a generic term for any sort of light, sport-weight yarn, and logically enough, a shawl made of this yarn was called a Shetland shawl. In her book *Our Life in the Highlands,* Queen Victoria mentions meeting a very excellent Shetland shawl knitter. Mary Thomas, when she uses the term "Shetland shawl" in her amazingly complete *Mary Thomas's Knitting Book,* does distinguish between the very fine lace shawls and the plainer Shetland everyday shawls; she cites seamless construction as the hallmark of the real thing.

Over time, the knitted shawl slowly shifted from fashionable to traditional garb. Norbury reports that the last Mrs. Hunter on Unst died in about 1960 at the age of eighty-one, leaving her last shawl, a museum-quality piece, to the collection of a large British wool firm. In 1980, Sarah Don reports the existence of a Mrs. Peterson, the only woman on Unst capable of spinning the super-fine wool for Shetland lace shawls. Among handspinners in North

Blocking Shetland shawls on drying frames in the Shetland Islands, late 19th century.

America in the 1980s and 90s, there has been an encouraging revival of fine spinning. Current fine spinners are now producing yarns that measure up to the old Shetland standards; master knitters are also meeting the challenge of similarly fine lacework.

Fortunately, openwork and lace shawls are still much admired and preserved in Scotland. In 1985, I saw a beautiful small collection of antique Shetland lace shawls at the large woolen mill in St. Andrew; here customers could purchase everything needed to knit their own (even a spinning wheel)! Knowing my interest, friends continue to bring me "Shetland shawl" knitting leaflets from Wales and Scotland. A recent one, ironically titled *Real Shetland Shawl,* involves knitting the edging separately and sewing it on—something a "real Shetland shawl" maker would never do. The leaflets do show, however, that craft publishers and yarn manufacturers perceive an enduring interest in traditional shawl-making on the part of their knitting customers.

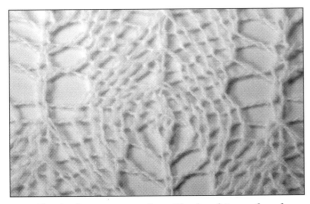

Detail, Fir Cone pattern in a Shetland Lace shawl knitted by the author.

SHAWL MATERIALS

YARN OPTIONS

The best knitted shawls are both light and warm, though they may be five to six feet (1.5 to 1.8 meters) across. Therefore, shawl knitters must use thin, lightweight yarns. Heavy yarns (such as three- or four-ply worsted-weight yarns, bulky-weight, or Lopi yarns) are best used for winter caps, sweaters, or afghans. Sport-weight yarns are the heaviest that may be used for shawls. Handspun or commercial singles or soft-spun two-ply yarns are excellent choices. Many of the yarns sold on cones for weaving or machine knitting are suitable, as are mill-end cones from commercial knitwear factories. In Scotland, several types of "laceweight" (generally, very light two-ply) yarns are still manufactured. Some of these are available from American importers or directly from Scottish sources.

In addition to wool yarns, lightweight cotton, silk, rayon, linen, ramie, synthetics, or blends are also good choices for shawls. However, some of these yarns may be too weighty unless the shawl is small or includes a great deal of openwork. Think of the weight of your favorite cotton sweater and imagine it in the size of a shawl.

Synthetic yarns deserve mention. Because they are inexpensive and widely available, they are excellent for experimentation—you'll have few qualms throwing away stunted, misshapen sample swatches made of yarn that costs little. But because many synthetic yarns do not block well, they may not be a good choice for the final piece. Much of the beauty of knitted openwork depends on good blocking. This beauty may be lost if the yarn will not remain stretched when it dries. If you want to use a synthetic yarn, block a sample first to make sure it will keep

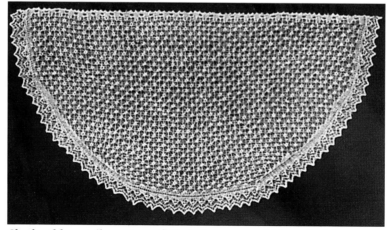

Shetland lace veil courtesy of Chris Bunyan and Mary Smith,
A Shetland Knitter's Notebook.

its blocked shape. Then choose your shawl design accordingly. Don't spend hours knitting an openwork design that will never be seen.

Buy the best yarn you can afford and choose colors and fibers that please your eye and hand. These yarns will be used, admired, and enjoyed, while sale bargains and "almost rights" may never leave the closet. If possible, look at yarns in natural light when choosing colors. Avoid fluorescent lights, which have limited color spectrums that can alter the appearance of the yarn.

Estimating yardage

How much yarn is required for a shawl? I generally estimate between eight and eighteen ounces (about 227 to 510 grams), depending on the gauge, stitch pattern, yarn weight and thickness, shawl size, type of border, and even the patience of the knitter.

Eight ounces (227 grams) is appropriate for a triangle or rectangle of useable size, or a forty- to fifty-inch (101- to 127-centimeter) circle or square. An additional six to eight ounces (170 to 227 grams) will allow a sixty- to seventy-inch (152- to 178-centimeter) circle or square, or allow for a denser pattern or the addition of generous fringe to a triangle or rectangle. Sixteen to eighteen ounces (454 to 510 grams) of yarn will produce a shawl measuring a generous six feet (1.8 meters) across—about as large as can be worn easily and an admirable size for napping!

These amounts may be inexact. Shawls can accommodate the amount of yarn you have on hand, rather than vice-versa. The amount you need for a shawl is not nearly so crucial as the amount you need for a fitted garment. Most shawl designs allow you to knit until your yarn or desire runs out.

So be generous when planning for a shawl, but do not get overly concerned with amount. Any yarn leftover will eventually come in handy, and a border can always be added to enlarge a shawl that turns out smaller than you'd like.

If you know how to spin a useable singles or thin two-ply, you can make your own yarn, as has been done for centuries. In fact, if you are an accomplished spinner, you may be able to make yarns even finer than those commercially available. In such cases, less than eight ounces (227 grams) of yarn may be all that's required. Some of the very finest Shetland lace shawls have been made from handspun and weigh less than four ounces (113 grams). In spinning your own yarn for a shawl, not only will you have a respectable accomplishment in itself, you'll also have the pleasure of continuing the long and honored tradition of knitting with your own handspun.

TOOLS

Few tools are needed for shawl knitting and those required are fairly inexpensive and completely portable. The primary tools are knitting needles, both circular and double-pointed. Most shawls become far too large to be worked on straight needles, and besides, even for flat knitting, circular needles work better. They distribute the weight of the knitting in the center of your lap, can (in longer lengths) easily accommodate hundreds of stitches, won't fall to the floor accidentally, and will save your seatmate (on plane or sofa) from being poked in the ribs, or worse. There is nothing mysterious about circular needles—use them just as you would straight needles. If the flexible nylon cable connecting the tips of circular needles kinks, simply pour very hot water over it, and straighten while it's still warm and pliable. (This trick can be used for bent plastic needles as well.)

Double-pointed needles are needed only for the first few rounds of square or circular shawls worked from the center outward. Although these beginning rows can be maddening, they have so few stitches that the work progresses quickly past the slippery part. Knitting guru Meg Swansen recommends using wooden or bamboo needles which are less slick than metal and help prevent stitches from slipping off. Don't let these few difficult rows discourage you from knitting shawls from the center outward—such shawls are probably the most fun and versatile, and very likely the most beautiful, you'll ever knit.

Double-pointed needles are sold in sets of four and sets of five. If possible, buy them in sets of five. It is much easier to divide your work into quarters (four needles) and knit with a fifth, than to arrange your work into thirds (three needles) and knit with a fourth. If you cannot find sets of five needles, buy two sets of four needles. You'll have a fifth to knit with, and a few spares that may come in handy for knitting gloves or replacing a lost needle.

Other useful tools

Other useful tools are listed below in order of importance.

Stitch markers. For keeping track of pattern sections and the beginning of the round.

Blunt-end needle. For weaving in yarn ends, etc.

Crochet hooks. For picking up dropped stitches or making crocheted borders. I find that size E (3.5 mm) and J (5.5 mm) are suitable for most jobs.

Waste yarn. For holding stitches.

Scissors. For cutting yarn in multicolored patterns.

Tape measure. For measuring your progress.

Point protectors. For preventing stitches from falling off the needles when not in use.

Calculator. For calculating the number of stitches needed for patterns.

If you work with handspun or yarns that are put up in cones or twisted hanks, you may find an umbrella swift and ball winder useful. The rotating swift stretches and holds the hank while the ball winder winds the yarn into a convenient center-pull ball. Both clamp to a table, chair, or stool.

Designing Shawls

Designing your own shawls is as easy as making the following determinations:

Function. What is the purpose of this shawl? Who will wear it or use it?

Shape. What shape will best suit the shawl's purpose?

Size. What size will best suit the shawl's purpose? About how much yarn will it take to make the appropriate size shawl?

Fiber. What fiber is best for this shawl? Wool, cotton, acrylic, silk, rayon, mohair, linen, or a blend? What's available?

Weight. What weight of yarn or fiber will best suit this shawl? (Cotton and linen, for example, usually weigh more per yard than silk or wool. Synthetics are lightweight.)

Color. What color(s) will suit this shawl? What's available? Of these, what will suit me or the intended wearer?

Pattern. What stitch pattern will create the texture I want? What stitch pattern will be compatible with the weight and color of my chosen yarn?

Finish. How shall I finish the shawl? Given the size, shape, yarn, color, and stitch pattern, what will be best—a plain border, crocheted loops, fringe, or an edging?

You may already have the answers to some of these questions. For example, if you use yarn on hand, you know the fiber, weight, and color. The answers to other questions you may not know. For example, you may not know what color shawl your cousin would like for her new baby or exactly how much yarn is needed for an oversized bed covering. But that's part of the fun of designing. Fortunately, the more you do it, the better you become.

WORKING WITHOUT WRITTEN INSTRUCTIONS

For those accustomed to row-by-row instructions, the hardest part of shawl making is integrating the shaping with the stitch patterns. Don't despair; most shawl shapes follow a simple formula. You can familiarize yourself with shapings by making plain shawls without fancy stitch patterns. If the thought of large, plain shawls bores you, consider making miniature shawls. You'll learn as much by knitting doll-sized shawls as their full-sized counterparts, but you'll invest far less in time and materials.

Incorporating stitch patterns

Once you're familiar with shaping methods, it's easy to incorporate a stitch pattern. You can greatly simplify matters by deciding on the number of stitches to start with. If the stitch pattern repeats over an even number of stitches, begin with an even number of stitches. If the stitch pattern repeats over an odd number, begin with an odd number. The difference between an even and odd number is just one stitch, so this adjustment will not affect the overall look of the shawl, especially when you're in charge of the design.

Work a few plain (stockinette) stitches adjacent to the shaping increases and mark the beginning and end of the stitch pattern sections to help set them off. As the shawl progresses, the plain and shaping stitches will frame the pattern stitches and blend into the overall design. (In fact, you can work quite a lot of a shawl in stockinette stitch without compromising its appearance; a shawl need not be entirely patterned.)

Planning for increases

Charting stitches on graph paper will help you design shawls and keep track of tricky parts. Chart one section of the shawl from shaping increase to shaping increase—one quarter of a square shawl, for instance, or one pie-shaped section of a circular or semicircular shawl. Triangular and rectangular shawls can be charted in their entirety, or as one section that is repeated throughout. For practice, use the symbols on page 111 to chart the stitches of the center row or round in one corner of the graph paper. Then add the stitches for the next row or round, then the next, according to the shaping and stitch patterns you have decided on. (Starting in a corner of the paper allows space for the expanding pattern.) If you like, use different colors to discern different rows or rounds. After you've charted just one or two pattern repeats, you'll be able to see how the pattern stitch combines with the shaping increases.

If you plan to combine several stitch patterns, you may find it helpful to write out row-by-row instructions for each stitch on an index card. This will allow you to read the entire pattern at a glance. For added clarity, write instructions for the even-numbered rows in one color and the odd-numbered rows in another. The simple act of writing out the instructions will help you focus on how the pattern develops. If you imagine knitting each row as you write it, you'll be familiar with the pattern before you begin knitting.

GAUGE

Gauge is the number of stitches per inch (2.5 cm) knitted with a specific size needle, a specific yarn, and a particular stitch pattern. Gauge is unique to each knitter—no one can determine your gauge for you because no one knits with exactly the same tension on the yarn.

To achieve a light, springy, drapeable fabric suitable for a shawl, the gauge must be larger and looser than what you use for sturdy garments such as socks, gloves, or sweaters. A knitted shawl should never be tight or stiff. Its "hand" (how it feels in your hand) should be soft, flexible, flowing, and crushable.

You can alter your gauge by adjusting your needle size. Given the same yarn, stitch pattern, and knitter, larger needles will result in fewer stitches per inch and a looser fabric; smaller needles will produce a firmer fabric and more stitches.

Most shawls work up best at a gauge of about three stitches per inch, depending on the yarn weight. For many knitters, this requires a surprisingly large needle size of 7 to 10½ (4.5 to 6.5 mm). However, the actual gauge is much less important than the hand of the knitted fabric. Your goal is to achieve the ideal fabric, not a predetermined number of stitches per inch.

Sampling for correct gauge and drapeability.

Sampling

Different stitch patterns demand different hands. When you've chosen a stitch pattern, knit a sample swatch to determine the best needle size. Knit one swatch with the smallest needle you think may work and another swatch with the largest. For example, a garter-stitch lace pattern worked in wool singles should be stretchy and light. Such a fabric will be possible with a needle size of 6 to 10 (4 to 6 mm). Knit a swatch with each size and compare the two. If the fabric worked with the larger needle is too flimsy, and the one worked with the smaller is too stiff, then try another swatch with an intermediate needle size.

Although many knitters work with gauge swatches that measure four inches (10 cm) square, this is generally too small for determining gauge for a shawl. At an average of three stitches per inch, such a swatch would consist of only twelve stitches. For shawls, I recommend using at least twenty stitches, or a minimum of one, and preferably two, pattern repeats in both stitches and rows.

For example, a sample swatch for a twelve-stitch pattern repeat should have at least twenty-four stitches (two pattern repeats). At a gauge of three stitches per inch, twenty-four stitches will make an eight-inch (20.5-cm) wide swatch—twice the standard size! This will give you a good idea of the pattern's appearance and hand. Moreover, swatching two repeats in both width and length will acquaint you with the pattern before you begin your shawl.

You can unravel the gauge swatch and reuse the yarn or save the swatch for future reference. A saved swatch ensures that you'll have yarn on hand if the shawl should ever require mending.

In some cases, you may want to use more than one needle size. For example, combining two (or more) yarns that differ in weight may necessitate two needle sizes to produce an even gauge and smooth fabric. If you want the center of a square or circular shawl to be firm and the edges to be soft and open, you may want to work the two parts with different needles. In most cases, a difference of one or two sizes won't affect your gauge drastically, but it may be just what's needed for the effect you want.

How to knit and use a gauge swatch

Work a gauge swatch with the yarn, needles, and stitch pattern that you plan to use for your shawl. To prevent curling, work a few garter stitches on each edge.

To work the swatch, cast on at least three stitches for the left edge, twenty to twenty-five stitches (at least one pattern repeat) for the swatch, and another three stitches for the right edge. The exact number of stitches will depend on your yarn, needles, stitch pattern, and tension. Work one to two pattern repeats (or at least fifteen to twenty rows), working the edge stitches in garter stitch. Remove the swatch from the needles and pin it (as is for textured patterns or stretched for openwork patterns) to a flat surface. Place a straight pin next to one stitch, measure across two inches (5 cm), and place another pin. Count the number of stitches, including partial stitches, between the two pins. Divide this number in half to determine the number of stitches per inch. Do the same in the vertical direction, placing the first pin at the base of a stitch, to determine the row gauge.

Determining the number of stitches and rows for your shawl

Once you know your stitch and row gauge, you can determine the number of stitches you'll need for a particular width of fabric by multiplying the desired width in inches (cm) by the number of stitches per inch (cm):

(desired width) × (number of stitches per inch) = number of stitches.

The number of rows you'll need to knit for a particular length is figured the same way:

(desired length) × (number of rows per inch) = number of rows.

Note: Some stitch patterns, such as cables or ribbing, contract or draw together. Compared to the same number of stitches worked in stockinette stitch, these patterns will be narrower than expected. Other stitch patterns, such as openwork or lace patterns, expand and become wider than the same number of stitches worked in stockinette stitch. Therefore, to ensure that your shawl ends up the size you intend, make a separate gauge swatch for each stitch pattern you plan to use in a large area of knitting.

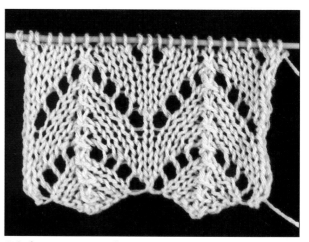

Stitch pattern swatch.

SHAPING SHAWLS

TRIANGLES

In addition to triangular, shawls can be square, rectangular, circular, or half-circular. You can think of all these shapes as composed of triangles. Therefore, it makes sense to learn how to shape a triangle first. This knowledge will provide the foundation for all other shawl shapes.

Triangular shawls are worked back and forth in rows. Those worked from the point to the wide edge are easy to shape. You begin with just one or two stitches, and the finished size need not be predetermined—you can knit until your yarn or patience runs out! If you were to work your triangle the other way, from the wide edge to the tip, not only would you have to decide on the finished size in advance to know how many stitches to cast on, but you would then have to cast on those hundreds of stitches and knit that gigantic first row with even tension and without losing any stitches. Moreover, you would have to continue until all those stitches had been decreased to form the tip—you couldn't quit or run out of yarn, or your shawl would be pointless!

I use two ways to shape a triangular shawl with one square (ninety-degree angle) corner and two half-square (forty-five-degree angle) corners. I call one method "tip-to-tip" and the other "tip-to-top".

Tip-to-tip triangle

This triangle is worked sideways from point to point. Cast on one or two stitches (depending whether there is an odd or even number of stitches

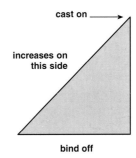

Tip-to-tip method for triangles.

in the pattern repeat), and increase one stitch at the end of every other row. When the piece is the length you want, bind off all stitches.

Because increased stitches form one edge of this triangle and bound-off stitches another, the two may vary in length and evenness. Therefore, this method may result in a less-than-perfect triangle.

Tip-to-top triangle

This triangle is worked from the point to the long edge or base. Cast on one or two stitches and increase one stitch at the beginning and end of every other row. When the piece is the length you want, bind off all stitches. Unlike the tip-to-tip triangle, increases are worked simultaneously on both sides and produce a more symmetrical shape.

Theoretically, you could create a triangular shape by working the two lines of increases down the center of the shawl, rather than at each edge. In practice, though, doing so would make the top edge of the triangle curve.

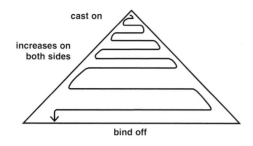

Tip-to-top method for triangles.

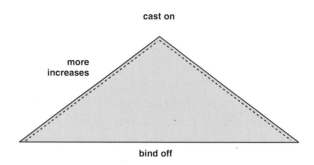

A faster rate of increase makes a wider triangle.

The rate of increase is the ratio of increases made to rows worked. By altering the rate of increase, you can alter the shape of the triangle. Working more increases more frequently will cause the edges to stretch out and the top to widen. Working fewer increases less frequently will produce shorter edges and a narrower top.

You can evaluate how a specific rate will affect the final shape by laying a protractor against the tip of a knitted test triangle and extrapolating the angle between the edges . By adjusting the rate of increase, you can produce exactly the shape you want.

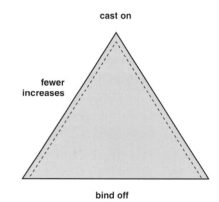

A slower rate of increase makes a narrower triangle.

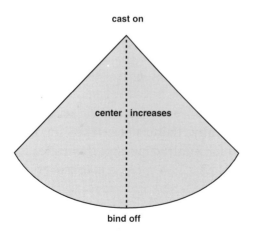

Center, rather than side increases create a 'humped' triangle.

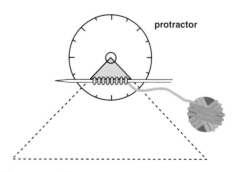

Checking rate of increase.

Increases

The way you choose to increase is up to you—it's part of the design process. You can increase by casting on one stitch, knitting and then purling in the same stitch, knitting into the front and back of a stitch, knitting into the stitch or bar below the stitch on the needle, or by working a yarn-over. In part, the method to choose may depend on your stitch pattern. For example, an openwork pattern typically involves yarn-overs; openwork is also appropriate for shaping increases. Garter-stitch patterns will look better with a more invisible increase such as casting on a stitch or knitting into the front and back of a stitch.

To help you keep track of increase rows, use a row counter. If you increase every other row, put a colored dot on one needle tip or use two colors of straight needles and increase every time the marked needle is in your right hand. Such color coding is especially helpful when the two increase points are separated by a huge number of stitches.

Incorporating stitch patterns

You can incorporate a multitude of patterns (see pages 33–68) into triangular shawls. But keep in mind that many patterns, especially those with large amounts of stockinette stitch, will curl at the edges. If the stitch pattern you choose does curl, add a substantial border, either simultaneously or after the center of the shawl is complete. A traditional solution is to stitch a wide lace edging to a somewhat plain center.

To prevent curling, use a stitch pattern that contains a fairly even mix of knit and purl stitches (such as seed stitch, sand stitch, Irish moss stitch, basketweave stitch, or the many rib stitches) or one that has a garter-stitch foundation. Many traditional triangular shawls are knitted entirely in plain garter or an open garter stitch. Usually a combination of fine yarn and large needles can produce a surprisingly light and open garter-stitch fabric. Many traditional Shetland lace stitches, such as the popular Old Shale pattern, are worked on a garter-stitch background. This is not surprising considering that the original Shetland lace shawls were worked back and forth on double-pointed needles (before circular needles were manufactured), and stitches other than garter were too loose to hold the needles. In addition, a garter-stitch background eliminates time-consuming purling and prevents curling.

SQUARES

Most traditional knitted shawls, including many of the famous Shetland lace shawls, are square. They were probably modeled after their woven counterparts, which were traditionally square or twice-square (a rectangle twice as long as wide). The square shape is handy for wrapping a baby, spreading over a bed, or wearing.

Traditional Shetland square

Before circular needles were available, large knitted pieces had to be worked on straight needles. Consequently, knitters developed an ingenious method for constructing large shawls that involved very little binding off. The resulting shawl was soft and elastic.

However, this method required a tremendous amount of grafting—a tricky operation made more complicated by the use of lace-weight yarn. To make the grafted seams light and unnoticeable, a row of

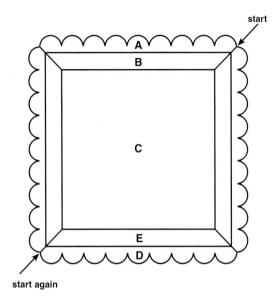

Traditional Shetland Shawl shaping. Cast on first edging A. 1. Knit back and forth, making cast-on and bind off edges mitered. 2. Along straight edge of edging, pick up stitches for first border B. Knit border back and forth, decreasing along both edges and continuing to miter corners. 3. Knit center section C back and forth. Leave stitches on needle. 4. Cast on second edging D, and knit it and then second border E, as in 1 and 2. Graft border to C stitches still on needle. 5. Make side edging and border sections, and graft them to center selvedges and to first and second borders at corners.

yarn-overs was worked on the last row of each section to be grafted. Where sections of the shawl were picked up, a set of false holes (yarn-overs) was worked so that the picked-up sections would match the grafted sections.

Another disadvantage to this method is that the finished size must be predetermined—the length of the first edging determines the size of the square.

Seamless square

Thanks to the manufacture of circular needles, we can now knit a soft shawl without seams, bind-off edges, or grafting. Like the triangular shawl worked from tip to top, a circular-knit square shawl is worked in a single piece. It is perfectly proportioned and can be as large as desired without much preplanning. You need only reserve a few balls of yarn for the final edging. In a pinch, you can usually work a crocheted loop edging with just one large ball of yarn.

For a circular-knit square, simultaneously work four ninety-degree triangles (made by increasing one stitch per edge every other row) side by side from the points outward.

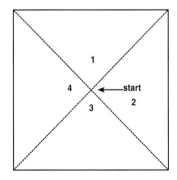

Square formed from four triangles.

Center-started square

A square shawl worked in the round requires five double-pointed needles, one for each quarter-section and a fifth for knitting. If you don't have a set of five needles, you can combine two similar sizes, such

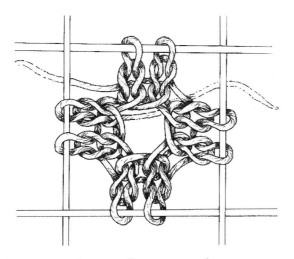

Center started square, first two rounds.

as two size 7 (4.5 mm) and three size 8 (5 mm) needles. Begin the square as follows:

Round 1: Cast on 8 stitches and place 2 stitches onto each of 4 needles. This is easier said than done! You may find it helpful to work over a table or desk—let the needles rest on the top. As you manipulate them, try to keep them in a square shape, and in the same order as the cast-on sequence. Try not to let them twist or flip over.

Round 2: Join into a round and knit.

Round 3: Using the increase method of your choice, increase in or after every stitch to double the number of stitches—4 stitches on each of 4 needles.

Round 4: Knit.

Round 5: Begin the lines of increase by increasing 1 stitch at the beginning and end of each of 4 needles—6 stitches on each needle (each quarter-section); 24 stitches total. Note: If you choose to increase with yarn-overs, work the increases 1 stitch in from the edges to avoid dropped increases. The increases will separate the quarter-sections visually so that when you move to a circular nee-

dle, it will be easier to keep track of the increase points.

Round 6: Knit.

Round 7: Same as Round 5, increase 1 stitch on each side of each quarter-section—8 stitches on each needle; 32 stitches total.

Round 8: Knit.

Continue alternating increase rounds (2 stitches increased at each corner; 8 stitches increased total) with plain rounds. When the stitches become too crowded on the double-pointed needles, change to a short circular needle (see page 113), placing markers at the four corners to mark the lines of increase. You may find it helpful to mark the beginning of the round with a contrasting marker. When the stitches

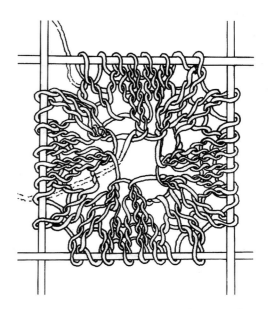

Center started square, seventh round. Lines of increase established with yarn-overs.

are too crowded on the short needle, change to a longer one. When the shawl is the desired size, bind off all stitches—that's all there is to it!

Bordered square

A square shawl can also be made by knitting back and forth for the center and then picking up stitches around each of the four sides with a circular needle and knitting the border in the round. This method requires a bit more planning if you want a shawl of a specific size or have a limited amount of yarn. Because it's difficult to account for blocking in determining the finished dimensions, make generous test swatches of both the center and border stitch patterns. Measure the swatches after they've been blocked to determine the number of stitches you'll need to arrive at the size you want.

The center square can be worked two ways—side to side or on the bias. A square knit from side to side has no shaping and can easily be worked in a pattern stitch. To determine when the piece is the correct shape, fold it along the diagonal so that one selvedge edge is parallel with the last row knitted. The piece is perfectly square if the cast-on edge lies directly on top of and even with the other selvedge edge.

Working the center square on the bias, from one corner to the other, is the more traditional method,

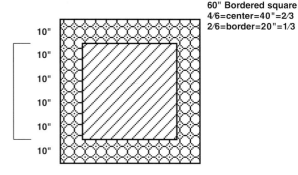

60" Bordered square
4/6=center=40"=2/3
2/6=border=20"=1/3

10"
10"
10"
10"
10"
10"
10"

Bordered square, 2/3 to 1/3 proportion.

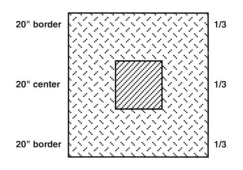

20" border   1/3

20" center   1/3

20" border   1/3

Bordered square equal thirds proportions.

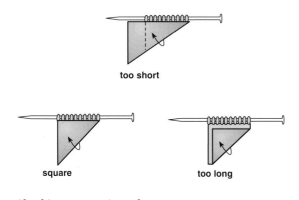

too short

square   too long

Checking proportion of square.

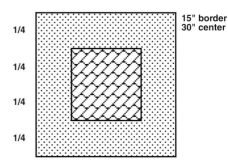

1/4

1/4

1/4

1/4

15" border
30" center

Bordered square quarter portions.

and is most easily done in plain or patterned garter stitch. To knit a square on the bias, proceed as you would for a triangle, increasing on each edge, until you reach the center, and then decrease on each edge proportionally for the other half.

The relative sizes of the center and border are up to you. A popular ratio is for the center square to make up two-thirds of the overall length (or width) and the border to make up one-third. For example, a 60-inch (152-cm) shawl would have a 40-inch (102-cm) center and a 10-inch (25-cm) border on each side.

Probably the most difficult task in knitting this type of shawl is picking up stitches for the border. The same number of stitches must be picked up on each side of the center square if the border is to be even. Although this can be done "by eye", it is helpful to divide each side into halves or quarters, and then pick the same number of stitches within each of these smaller sections. To pick up stitches around a center square worked on the bias, knitting legend Elizabeth Zimmermann suggests picking up three stitches for every two selvedge loops.

Place a marker at the beginning of the round and join. On the first round, place markers on either side of each corner stitch (or two corner stitches). Increase one stitch at each marker every other round, just as you would increase for a center-started square.

Treat the border for each side of the square separately, and center the pattern stitch separately within each. Work the corner stitches and a few stitches on either side in stockinette stitch. Work the increased stitches in the pattern stitch when there are enough stitches to work a complete repeat. For additional tips on adding pattern stitches, see the next section.

Finish the shawl as you wish—with fringe, a crocheted-off edge, or a knit-on border or edging. See page 69 for techniques.

Incorporating stitch patterns

You can add a pattern stitch to each section of a square shawl as soon as you have increased enough stitches to accommodate the pattern repeat. Remember to increase two stitches in each section every other round. You can start a pattern that repeats over four or five stitches after just six or seven rounds of knitting, which will add interest to the center of the shawl. A pattern that repeats over a large number of stitches requires you to first work many more increase rounds.

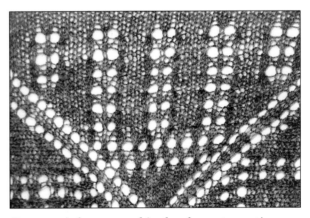

Pattern stitches centered in shawl quarter-section.

Only begin a stitch pattern when there are enough stitches for a full pattern repeat, excluding the stitches used along the lines of increase. Leave those stitches alone! Their job is to form the square; yours is to embellish the stitches in between with patterns. As you increase stitches on either side of the first pattern repeat, work them in stockinette stitch. Continue to work them in stockinette stitch

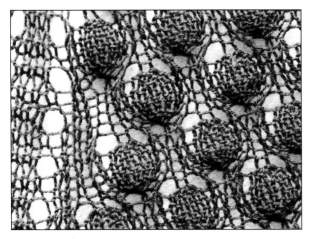

Plain knit-stitch edges blend with new motifs after increasing.

until there are enough to work another full pattern repeat. These plain stitches will blend into the overall design and help you keep track of the shaping increases .

For simplicity, choose a pattern stitch in which every other row is purled. These "rows" will be knitted when worked in the round. If you begin the stitch pattern on a shaping/increase round, you can simply knit every other round even. This will help you keep track of when to work the shaping increases.

For eye-pleasing symmetry, center the pattern within each section. To center a pattern, work the center stitch of the section according to the center stitch of the repeat. There should be the same number of plain stitches on each side of the pattern stitches. If the stitch pattern repeats over an even number of stitches, there must be an even number of stitches in each section. If the pattern repeats over an odd number of stitches, there must be an odd number. If necessary, simply increase or decrease one stitch at the center of each section (to avoid entanglement with the shaping lines of increase) to change from an odd number of stitches to an even number, or vice-versa. One stitch more or less will have little impact on the shape of the square, but it will greatly affect the success of the stitch pattern.

If you want, you can change pattern stitches as you go. Traditionally, different pattern stitches are delineated with a few rounds of stockinette stitch, reverse stockinette stitch (purl every round), or a round of openwork holes (*yarn-over, knit two stitches together; repeat from * around). If you prefer, you can simply allow each pattern to blend into the next.

Because it's not unusual to miss an increase or work an extra one here or there, periodically count the stitches in each section (count twice to be sure) and make note of them. On the next plain-knit round, even out any discrepancies by working invisible increases and/or decreases as needed, being careful not to interfere with the line-of-increase stitches or the pattern in progress. If you do this when you change from one pattern stitch to another, you can make adjustments for changing from an odd- to an even-numbered repeat (or vice-versa) at the same time. Even the best knitter can gain or lose a few stitches when working with such large numbers of them, so don't worry about mistakes, just fix them.

For speed and ease of knitting, change to a longer circular needle when your stitches become crowded and no longer slide easily on the needle (see page 113). Overcrowded stitches have a tendency to leap off the needle every chance they get. Use large needle caps, or pull the needle ends forward, cross them, and push them into the knitting when laying your work aside. When you lay your knitting aside, note down where you are in the pattern so you'll know where to begin when you pick it up again, per-haps days later.

CIRCLES AND HALF-CIRCLES

Circular shawls do not have the long history of square shawls because they are the product of mod-ern circular needles. In the past, small projects such as doilies, motifs, and medallions could be worked on double-pointed needles, but larger pieces such as collars, yokes, caps, and large doilies were worked back and forth on straight needles, then joined into a circle with a seam. However, the hundreds of stitches required for circular shawls can only be knit easily with circular needles. Although half-circles are worked back and forth in rows, just as triangles are, they are also most conveniently made on circular needles, especially when they are large and weighty.

In terms of shaping, think of a circle as being made up of many equal-sized triangles, much like the wedges of a pie. A circle may include twelve, six-

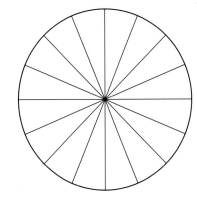

Circle formed by wedges.

teen, eighteen, or more narrow tip-to-top triangles, each made with two lines of increase worked at a slower rate than required for a square.

Remember that a square is made up of four nine-ty-degree triangles. If you superimpose this square over a circle composed of sixteen triangles, you'll see that each quarter of the square is composed of four narrow (22.5-degree) triangles. Therefore, to make a square into a circle, simply add more lines of increase and lessen the rate of increase. Instead of working four lines of increase, work sixteen; instead of increasing every other round, increase every fourth round.

Circle being knit on straight needles.

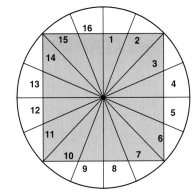

Relationship of square to circle.

Another way to shape a circle was conceived by Elizabeth Zimmermann for her 1969 Pi Shawl. Instead of working increases along lines that radiate outward from the center, she worked increases in rounds to form a sequence of circles within circles, like the ripples made by a stone thrown in a lake. In the illustration, each circle represents an increase round, a round in which the stitch count is doubled. The distance between increase rounds (the rate of increase) is increased progressively. This shaping is based on the formula circumference = πr^2. The number of stitches is doubled on each increase round and the distance between two increase rounds is double the distance between the previous two increase rounds.

I'll refer to these as the "rays" and the "rounds" methods of circle formation. Both produce flat-lying knitted circles that are begun at the center with double-pointed needles (see pages 20–21) and worked outward on circular needles as the stitch count increases.

Rays method of forming a circle

The rays method shapes a full-circle shawl by increasing two stitches every four rounds along each of sixteen lines that radiate outward from the center. Note that the following instructions are for shaping a shawl in stockinette stitch. You may also incorporate other stitch patterns.

Cast on two stitches onto each of four double-pointed needles—eight stitches total. Use a fifth needle to knit with. Place a marker and join, being careful not to twist stitches. See page 111 for abbreviations.

Rnd 1: Knit.
Rnd 2: *Inc 1, k1; rep from *—16 sts.
Rnds 3, 4, and 5: Knit.

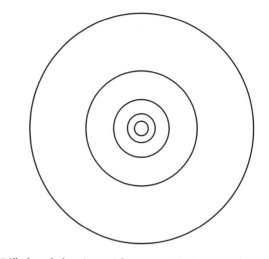

"Pi" shawl shaping with concentric increase lines.

Rnd 6: *Inc 2, k1; rep from *—48 sts.
Rnds 7, 8, and 9: Knit.
Rnd 10: *Inc 2, k3; rep from *—80 sts.
Rnds 11, 12, and 13: Knit.
Rnd 14: *Inc 2, k5; rep from *—112 sts.
Rnds 15, 16, and 17: Knit.
Rnd 18: *Inc 2, k7; rep from *—144 sts.
Rnds 19, 20, and 21: Knit.

Continue as established, increasing two stitches sixteen times every fourth round and working two more knit stitches between increase points each increase round.

Increases

There are several ways to "Inc 2":
A. YO, k1 from row below.
B. Cast-on 1, knit into front and back of next stitch.
C. Cast-on 1, k1 from row below.
D. YO, knit into front and back of next stitch.
E. K1 from bar below, then k1 from row below.

If you like, you can work a plain stitch between the two increase stitches. For example, work each of the sixteen triangles as follows: K1, inc 1, knit the center stitches, inc 1, k1. This would alter the round-by-round instructions above, but the shaping principle would remain the same.

Rays method of forming a half-circle

A half-circle made by the rays method is shown below. Two stitches are increased every four rounds along each of eight radiating lines. Note that a half-circle is worked back and forth in rows, not circularly in rounds. But there will be so many stitches, you'll want to use a circular needle.

Cast on 4 stitches.

Row 1: Knit.

Row 2: (RS) Using the method of your choice, inc in or after every st—8 sts.

Rows 3, 4, and 5: Knit. (Note that knitting every row forms garter stitch. You may also incorporate a different stitch.)

Rays method of increasing in progress.

Row 6: *Inc 2, k1; rep from *—24 sts.

Rows 7, 8, and 9: Knit.

Row 10: *Inc 2, k3; rep from *—40 sts.

Rows 11, 12, and 13: Knit.

Row 14: *Inc 2, k5; rep from *—56 sts.

Rows 15, 16, and 17: Knit.

Row 18: *Inc 2, k7; rep from *—72 sts.

Rows 19, 20, and 21: Knit.

Row 22: *Inc 2, k9; rep from *—88 sts.

Rows 23, 24, and 25: Knit.

Row 26: *Inc 2, k11; rep from *—104 sts.

Continue as established, increasing two stitches eight times every fourth row and working two more knit stitches between increase points each increase row until the piece is the desired size (about 250 to 300 stitches). Measure the length as you knit, but don't forget that blocking will increase the finished size.

Rounds method of forming a circle

To make a full-circle shawl by the rounds method of increase, you need only four double-pointed needles. The stitches are divided around three needles and the fourth is used for knitting. When the stitches become too crowded on the double-pointed needles, change to a circular needle (see page 113). Form the shape by doubling the number of stitches on increase rounds and increasing the space between the increase rounds geometrically. Note that the following instructions are for shaping a stockinette-stitch shawl. You may also wish to incorporate other stitch patterns.

Cast on 3 stitches onto each of 3 double-pointed needles—9 stitches total. Place a marker and join, being careful not to twist stitches.

Rnd 1: Knit.

Rnd 2: Using the method of your choice, inc 1 st in or after every st—18 sts.

Rnds 3, 4, and 5: Knit.

Rnd 6: Inc as before—36 sts.

Next 6 rnds: Knit.

Following Rnd: Inc as before—72 sts.

Next 12 rnds: Knit.

Following Rnd: Inc as before—144 sts.

Next 24 Rnds: Knit.

Following Rnd: Inc as before—288 sts.

Next 48 Rnds: Knit.

Following Rnd: Inc as before—576 sts.

Next 96 Rounds: Knit.

At some point during these 96 rounds, the shawl will probably be the size you want, though theoretically, you could continue indefinitely.

Rounds method of forming a half-circle

A half-circle made by the rounds method of shaping is knit back and forth. As with the rays method half-circle, the instructions below will produce a garter-stitch fabric.

These instructions are based on a multiple of five stitches; you can choose to use multiples of three, four, six, seven, or eight simply by casting on that number instead of five. If you do so, follow the instructions below, but note that your stitch count will be different.

Cast on 5 stitches.

Row 1: Knit.

Row 2: Using the method of your choice, inc 1 st in or after every st—10 sts.

Rows 3, 4, and 5: Knit.

Row 6: Inc as before—20 sts.

Next 6 Rows: Knit.

Following Row: Inc as before—40 sts.

Next 12 Rows: Knit.

Following Row: Inc as before—80 sts.

Next 24 Rows: Knit.

Following Row: Inc as before—160 sts.

Next 48 Rows: Knit.

Following Row: Inc as before—320 sts.

Next 96 Rows: Knit.

As with the full-circle version, this shawl will probably be the size you want at some point during these 96 rows, though you could continue indefinitely.

Practical tips for making half-circle shawls

The cast-on stitches for half-circle shawls form the center portion of the shawl's straight edge. The selvedge stitches form the remaining straight edge of the shawl, progressing outward from each side of the cast-on stitches. The stitches on the needle (or the bind-off edge when the piece is completed) form the curved edge of the half-circle.

Sizing

Most shawl wearers prefer shawls that are at least large enough to cover their "wingspan", the distance from one out-stretched hand to the other. To estimate the size of a half-circle shawl in progress, stretch out half the stitches over the needle while keeping a firm grip on the remaining stitches at the end. Measure the selvedge edge from the center of the cast-on stitches to the last stitch on the needle. This represents half the length of the straight edge, the part of the shawl that will rest along the wearer's shoulders and arms. Multiply this number by two to get the total width. Continue knitting until the top (straight) edge meets or exceeds the wearer's wingspan (better the shawl be too large than too small). The length of the shawl from neck to "hemline" will be half the top edge measurement—all rays of the circle will be the same length.

Wingspan measurement.

Introducing Stitch Patterns

Because half-circles are knitted back and forth in rows, choose stitch patterns that do not tend to curl. Garter stitch and garter-lace patterns are especially appropriate, but seed stitch or ribbing patterns work well, too.

Finishing

To prevent the selvedges from curling or the edges from stretching out of shape, most half-circle shawls require a border (the part that lies across the wearer's shoulders). You can work the border simultaneously with the main piece or, as I prefer, add it later by picking up stitches along the selvedge edges. I usually choose garter stitch, ribbing, or seed stitch for the border on a half-circle shawl.

Practical tips for making full-circle shawls

Like square shawls knit in the round, full-circle shawls made by either the rays or rounds shaping method have no selvedges so they do not curl at the edges. But you do have to take shaping methods into account when choosing stitch patterns.

Ray Style

Circles made by the rays method will have an even number of stitches in the total circumference but, for patterning, an odd number of stitches within each ray. One repeat of a pattern with a five-stitch multiple will fit into the ray after just a few rounds. When the center of the ray has increased to eleven stitches, two repeats of the pattern will fit, with one stitch left over. You can work that stitch between the two repeats or eliminate it for a few rounds by decreasing it. If you decrease it, add it in again when there are fourteen stitches at the center of the ray. Doing so will give you fifteen stitches, which will allow three pattern repeats. Work the increase stitches in stockinette stitch until there are enough to add one complete pattern repeat to each side of the ray.

Alternatively, you can create an even number of stitches at the center of the ray by increasing one stitch. Adding a stitch in the center will make the ray symmetrical and prevent entanglements with the shaping increases at the edges. To help avoid confusion, make such adjustments on shaping increase rounds so that all the increased stitches can be knit plain on the following round.

Some stitch patterns easily incorporated into the rays method of shaping a circle are Campanula, Feather Stitch, and Traditional Cat's Paw.

Rounds Style

Full-circle shawls made by the rounds shaping method are made up of concentric bands, each one wider than the last. These bands are ideal for stitch patterns. Because the shawls are begun with nine stitches, patterns that repeat over multiples of three stitches are the easiest to incorporate. But with a little figuring and stitch count adjustments, you can

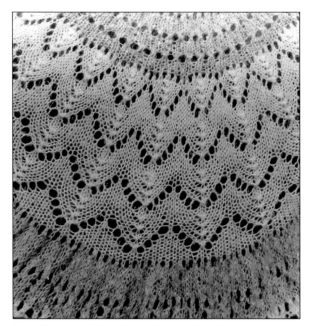

Detail, pattern bands in circular shawl.

incorporate a stitch pattern that has a ten-stitch repeat.

For example, if you have a total of 144 stitches and you want to incorporate a stitch pattern that repeats over ten stitches, you'll have four extra stitches (144 − 140 = 4). You can decrease those stitches in four places on the next round, or you can leave them alone and simply knit them in stockinette stitch. An easy way to distribute these four extra stitches is to work two of them at each of the halfway marks around the circle. Be sure to mark the pairs of extra stitches so that you don't continue the pattern stitch across them and throw the pattern off.

Some stitch patterns that can be used unaltered for the rounds method of making a circle are Willow, Herringbone Lace, Purse, Garter Lace, Horizontal Lace, St. John's Wort, Chevron Lace, and Old Shale.

RECTANGLES OR STOLES

Worked from the center

You can knit rectangles in the round as four triangles by using a slight variation of the square-shaping method. A four-triangle rectangle follows the same shaping principle as the four-triangle square, but uses two different shapes of triangles.

These triangles use the same four lines of increase, but the number of stitches and rate of increase in each quarter differ. A center-started rectangle may begin with ten stitches distributed on four needles as follows: two stitches, three stitches, two stitches, three stitches. The stitches for a rectangle that begins with eight stitches may be distributed one stitch, three stitches, one stitch, three stitches. The sections with more stitches will form wider triangles for the sides of the rectangle, the sections with fewer stitches will form narrower triangles for the ends.

Adjust the rate of increase for the ends to one stitch per line of increase every fourth round. Adjust the rate of increase for the sides to two stitches per

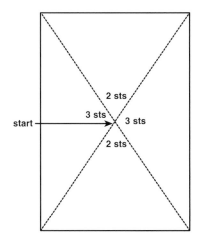

Shape from ten-stitch start.

line of increase every round for three rounds followed by no increases on the fourth round. This will widen the sides and narrow the ends of the triangular shapes.

Center cast-on variation

Another way to knit a rectangle in the round is to cast on enough stitches for two identical sides and a few stitches for each end. The two sides are knit straight and the increases are begun immediately on both sides of each end, forming the corners. The rate of increase is the same as for the triangle or square— two stitches per line of increase every other round. To help you keep track, mark the four lines of increases. Work this type of rectangular shawl on a circular needle, and when you finish the piece, carefully stitch together the center slit, matching stitch for stitch. (Alternatively, use a provisional cast-on for the side stitches and graft them together when you finish knitting.)

Worked end-to-end

In general, rectangles are most easily knit from one end to the other. For variation, knit a rectangle with edgings in the old Shetland lace style.

Cast on stitches for your lace edging and work it to the desired rectangle width. Bind off all stitches while working a row that goes back toward the flat side of the edging. Do not break the yarn, but pick up and knit stitches along the flat side of the edging for the body of the rectangle. Knit the rectangle to the desired length. Do not bind off the stitches. On the same needle, cast on the number of stitches required for the edging and work the edging back and forth in rows, working the last stitch of the edging together with the first stitch of the rectangle on every row of edging that connects with the rectan-

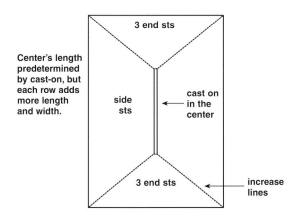

Rectangle knit in circular fashion. Relationship of length to width as rounds are added.

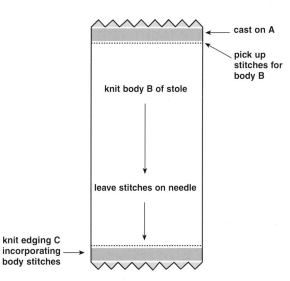

End-to-end stole. 1. Knit lace edging A. 2. Knit body of stole B from straight edge of A. Leave stitches on needle. 3. Cast on final edging C. Knit up stitches along straight edge of stole as you knit edging C. 4. Bind off edging.

gle. In so doing, you will knit the edging while binding off the rectangle. Bind off the edging stitches
when you've used all the stitches of the rectangle.

Incorporating stitch patterns

Many stitch patterns make beautiful stoles, and if
you plan to work back and forth, you can set the
width of a finished stole by the number of repeats of
the pattern it takes to make approximately the right
size. For example, if you want to use a stitch pattern
with an eight-stitch multiple and you want a stole
approximately thirty inches wide, use your stitch
gauge to determine how many stitches to cast on. If
your gauge is three stitches per inch, you'll need
ninety stitches to make a stole thirty inches wide.
However, because ninety isn't evenly divisible by
eight (the number of stitches in a pattern repeat),
there would be a partial repeat at one edge. By sim-

ply adjusting the number of stitches you cast on to a
multiple of eight, you can accommodate full pattern
repeats. In this case, adding six stitches would add
just two inches to the initial desired width, but
would eliminate the partial repeat. Altering the
stitch count in this manner will save you much figuring and re-thinking.

As with triangles and half-circles worked back
and forth, be cautious of stitch patterns that allow
selvedges to curl. You can prevent curling by working a border of seed or garter stitch simultaneously
with the rectangle. Such a border will also lend stability to the stole's edges. An alternative is to pick up
stitches after the rectangle is complete, as described
for a square (see pages 22–23).

Patterns for four-triangle rectangles knit in the
round are incorporated in the same way as their
square counterparts.

STITCH PATTERNS

OPENWORK PATTERNS

Most traditional shawls contain at least a little openwork, if only a narrow edging. Yarn-overs are the easiest of all increases to make, and they are the basis of all openwork stitch patterns.

You will nearly always find the yarn-over coupled with a decrease: k2tog; k2tog tbl; sl 1, k1, psso; or ssk. P2tog (on right, or more often wrong side of work) is also common. Some patterns pair two yarn-overs with a double decrease: sl 1, k2tog, psso. The aim of the paired increase and decrease is to create an openwork pattern while keeping the number of stitches the same. Sometimes the stitch numbers don't return to the starting number for a row or two, perhaps not even until a full repeat of pattern rows has been completed.

When working openwork, be aware that it will "open up" your stockinette or garter-stitch gauge, giving you fewer stitches to the inch and making the knitted fabric looser. But because openwork does not use more yarn—the yarn-overs take up space—openwork patterns are economical to knit.

Try a sample of the stitch pattern you're thinking of using to see just how much the gauge is affected. It is wise to knit at least two repeats of a small pattern, and at least twenty stitches for your swatch. You'll become familiar with the pattern very quickly while knitting a swatch, and if you decide you don't like the pattern, you haven't lost much time.

See page 111 for abbreviations and symbols. When possible, the lace patterns are presented as charts.

MESH STITCH OPENWORK PATTERNS

Cat's Eye or Eyelet

Multiple of 4 sts
Note: End pattern with Row 2 or 4.

Work rep only when working in the rnd.

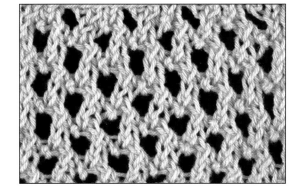

Purse Stitch

Multiple of 2 sts + 2.

end | ⌊rep⌋ | beg

Work rep only when working in the rnd.
Note: Work ⟋ as p2tog on both RS and WS rows

Bias Openwork

Multiple of 2 sts.

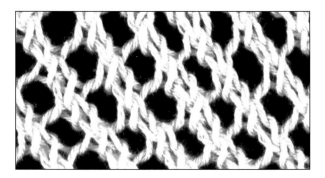

Madeira Bias

Multiple of 4 sts + 4.

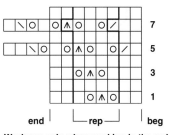

end | ⌊—rep—⌋ | beg

Work rep only when working in the rnd.

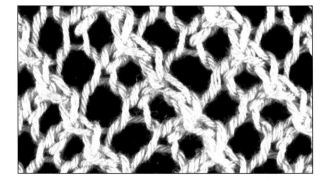

3 × 3 Leaf

Multiple of 6 sts + 2.

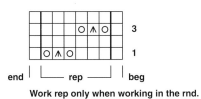

end | └─ rep ─┘ | beg

Work rep only when working in the rnd.

St. John's Wort

Multiple of 6 sts + 2.
Note: The yo in even-numbered rows falls between the k2 sts over which the slipped st has been passed.

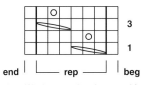

end | └─ rep ─┘ | beg

Work rep only when working in the rnd.

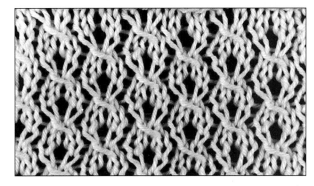

Campanula

Multiple of 5 sts + 2.
Note: This pattern draws in somewhat, like ribbing.

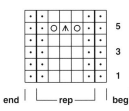

end | └─ rep ─┘ | beg

Work rep only when working in the rnd.

Herringbone Lace

Multiple of 6 sts + 2.

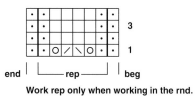

Work rep only when working in the rnd.

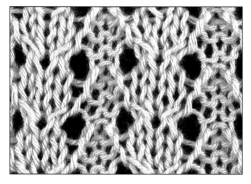

3 × 1 Herringbone

Multiple of 4 sts + 1.

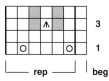

Work rep only when working in the rnd.

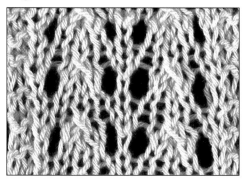

Mrs. Hunter's

Multiple of 4 sts + 2.

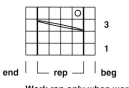

Work rep only when working in the rnd.

VERTICAL OPENWORK PATTERNS

Little Bells

Multiple of 14 sts.
Note: Twisted sts (k3 tbl, k1 tbl, etc.) make the "bells"
stand out against the purl background.

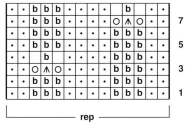

Van Dyke and Rib

Multiple of 12 sts + 5.

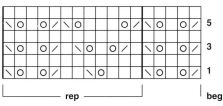

Work rep only when working in the rnd.

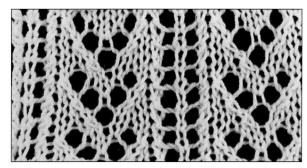

Twisted Rib Lace

Multiple of 6 sts + 1.

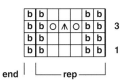

Work rep only when working in the rnd.

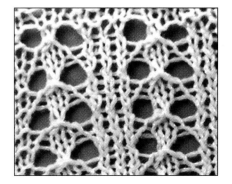

String of Beads

Multiple of 9 sts.

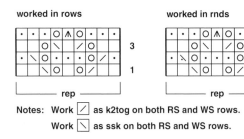

Notes: Work ⌐/⌐ as k2tog on both RS and WS rows.

Work ⌐\⌐ as ssk on both RS and WS rows.

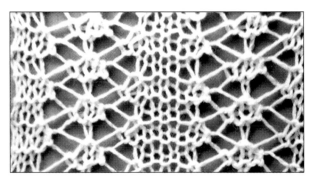

Traditional Cat's Paw

Multiple of 11 sts.

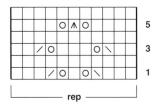

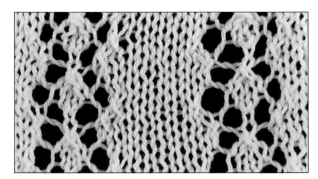

Narrow Cat's Paw

Multiple of 7 sts.

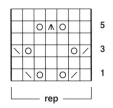

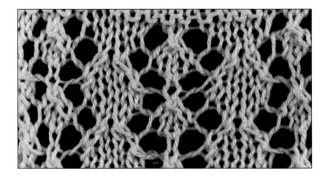

2 × 2 Openwork Rib

Multiple of 4 sts.

1

└─ rep ─┘

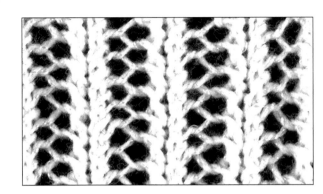

MEDIUM TO LARGE ALLOVER PATTERNS
(7 stitches or larger)

Traveling Vine

Multiple of 8 sts + 2.

Note: The twisted stitches (b) make a raised edge for the "vine".

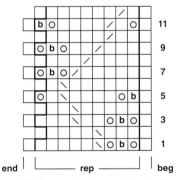

end ⎿─── rep ───⏌ beg

Work rep only when working in the rnd.

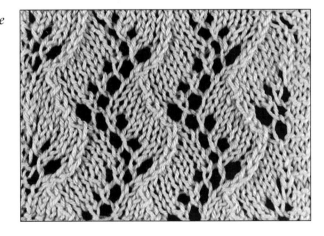

Snowdrop

Multiple of 8 sts + 5.

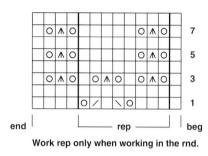

end — rep — beg

Work rep only when working in the rnd.

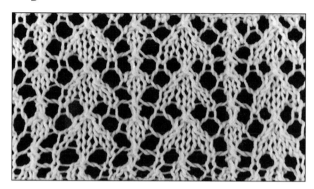

Shetland Leaves

Garter-based: *Multiple of 8 sts + 9.*
Stockinette based: *Multiple of 8 sts.*

Garter-based

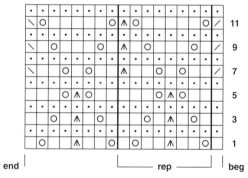

end — rep — beg

Work rep only when working in the rnd.

Stockinette-based

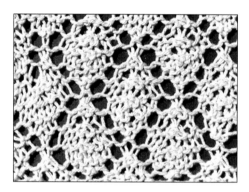

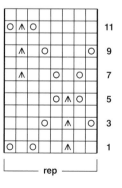

rep

Falling Leaves

Multiple of 10 sts + 6

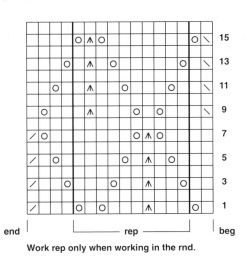

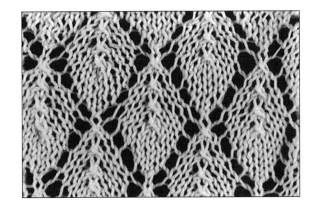

end   rep   beg

Work rep only when working in the rnd.

Wings of the Swan

Multiple of 23 sts + 2.

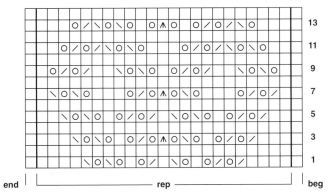

end   rep   beg

Work rep only when working in the rnd.

SMALL ALTERNATING OPENWORK PATTERNS

Butterfly

Multiple of 10 sts + 2.

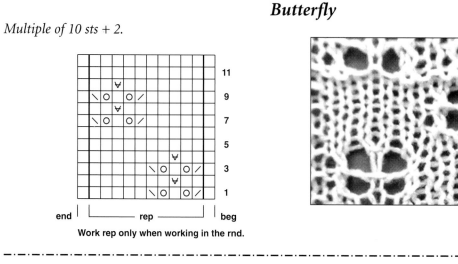

Work rep only when working in the rnd.

Alternating Feathers

Multiple of 6 sts + 1.
Note: End pattern with Row 12 or 24.

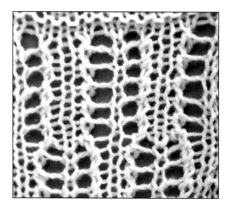

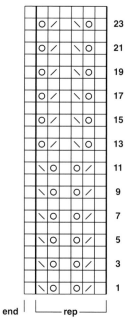

Work rep only when working in the rnd.

Broken Acre

Multiple of 10 sts + 2.
Note: End pattern with Row 8 or 16.

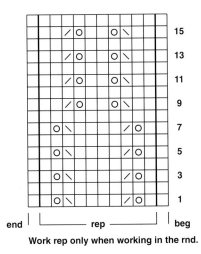

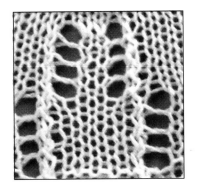

Work rep only when working in the rnd.

Dew Drop

Multiple of 6 sts + 7.
Note: This pattern has reverse stockinette stitch, but plenty of openwork; it lies flat and looks good on both sides.

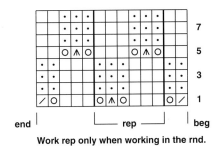

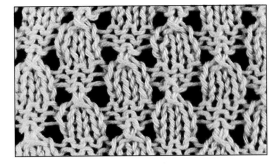

Work rep only when working in the rnd.

CHEVRON OPENWORK PATTERNS

Willow

Multiple of 10 sts + 13.

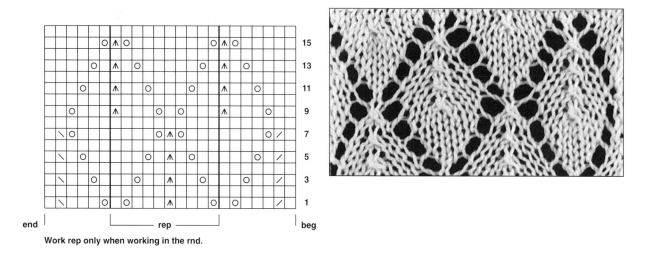

end | rep | beg

Work rep only when working in the rnd.

Chevron and Fagotting

Multiple of 8 sts + 1.

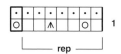

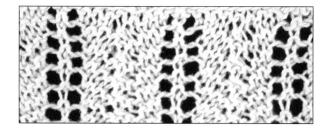

Chevron

Multiple of 6 sts + 2.

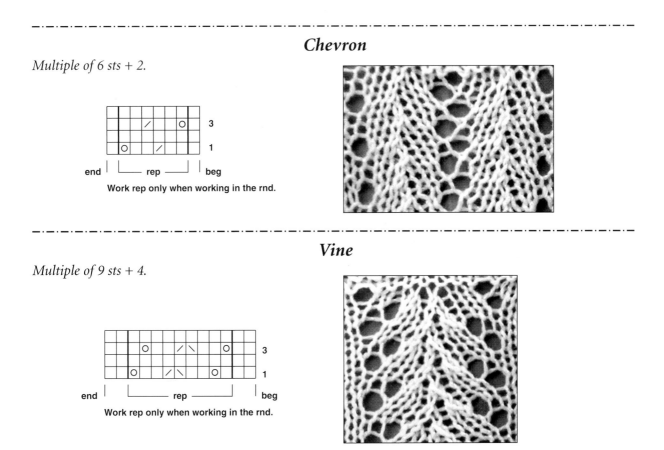

Work rep only when working in the rnd.

Vine

Multiple of 9 sts + 4.

Work rep only when working in the rnd.

TEXTURED STITCH PATTERNS

Textured stitch patterns make the warmest shawls. Use stitch patterns that are light and flexible. You can do this by using a looser, larger stitch gauge (fewer stitches per inch) and a lighter weight yarn than you would normally use for such patterns.

Textured stitch patterns can be successfully combined with openwork patterns to add extra warmth and substance to a shawl, or to add visual and tactile interest. Bands of textured pattern combine well with mesh openwork stitches such as Purse Stitch, Cat's Eye, or Bias Openwork.

Many textured patterns, such as Seed, Basketweave, Piqué Squares, and Irish Moss, are knit/purl combinations that look interesting on both sides. This makes the stitches especially suitable for half-circle, triangular, or rectangular shawls—shawls that are not folded so both sides are apt to show when worn. Reversible textured patterns are also non-curling, which is important to the back-and-forth knitting required by the half-circle, triangle, and rectangle.

Finally, textured stitches do not require blocking and are therefore ideal for unblockable synthetic yarns. Unlike openwork, textured stitches do not need to be stretched to show off their patterns. Also, because many synthetic yarns are lighter than natural fibers, a shawl of synthetic textured stitches may be surprisingly (and desirably) light.

Because these patterns are not lace, they are not charted.

SEED AND MOSS PATTERNS

Seed

In rows: *Any number of sts.*
Row 1: *K1, p1; rep from *.
Row 2: Knit the purl sts, purl the knit sts.
Repeat Row 2.

In rounds: *Uneven number of sts.*
Rnd 1: *K1, p1; rep from *.
Repeat Rnd 1.

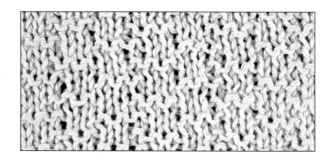

Seed Variation

In rows: *Multiple of 5 sts.*
Row 1: *P3, k2; rep from *.
Row 2 and 4: Purl.
Row 3: *P1, k2, p2; rep from *.
Repeat Rows 1–4.

In rounds: *Multiple of 5 sts.*
Rnd 1: *P3, k2; rep from *.
Rnds 2 and 4: Knit.
Rnd 3: *P1, k2, p2; rep from *.
Repeat Rnds 1–4.

Chevron Seed

In rows: *Multiple of 8 sts.*
Row 1: *P1, k3; rep from *.
Row 2: *K1, p5, k1, p1; rep from *.
Row 3: *K2, p1, k3, p1, k1; rep from *.
Row 4: *P2, k1, p1, k1, p3; rep from *.
Repeat Rows 1–4.

In rounds: *Multiple of 8 sts.*
Rnd 1: *P1, k3; rep from *.
Rnd 2: *K1, p1, k5, p1; rep from *.
Rnd 3: *K2, p1, k3, p1, k1; rep from *.
Rnd 4: *K3, p1, k1, p1, k2; rep from *.
Repeat Rnds 1–4.

Moss Dashes

In rows: *Multiple of 5 sts + 2.*
Row 1: K1, *p3, k2; rep from *, end k1.
Rows 2 and 4: Purl.
Row 3: K1, *p1, k2, p2; rep from *, end k1.
Repeat Rows 1–4.

In rounds: *Multiple of 5 sts.*
Rnd 1: *P3, k2; rep from *.
Rnds 2 and 4: Knit.
Rnd 3: *P1, k2, p2; rep from *.
Repeat Rnds 1–4.

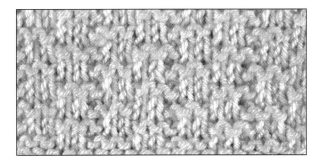

Double Moss

In rows: *Multiple of 4 sts.*
Rows 1 and 4: *K2, p2; rep from *.
Row 2 and 3: *P2, k2; rep from *.
Repeat Rows 1–4.

In rounds: *Multiple of 4 sts.*
Rnds 1 and 2: *K2, p2; rep from *.
Rnds 3 and 4: *P2, k2; rep from *.
Repeat Rnds 1–4.

Irish Moss

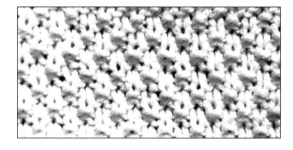

In rows: *Multiple of 2 sts.*
Rows 1 and 2: *K1, p1; rep from *.
Rows 3 and 4: *P1, k1; rep from *.
Repeat Rows 1–4.

In rounds: *Multiple of 2 sts.*
Rnds 1 and 4: *K1, p1; rep from *.
Rnds 2 and 3: *P1, k1; rep from *.
Repeat Rnds 1–4.

Dotted Rib

In rows: *Multiple of 2 sts.*
Row 1: *K1, p1; rep from *.
Row 2: Knit.
Repeat Rows 1–2.

In rounds: *Multiple of 2 sts.*
Rnd 1: *K1, p1; rep from *.
Rnd 2: Purl.
Repeat Rnds 1–2.

O AND V PATTERNS

_____

Trinity

Multiple of 2 sts + 2.

end | └ rep ┘ | beg

Work rep only when working in the rnd.

Note: Work ⟈ as p1, k1, p1 on even rnds.

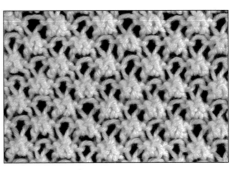

_____

Seafoam

Multiple of 16 sts.

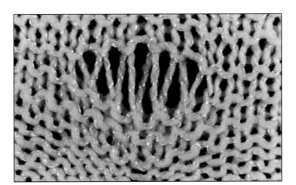

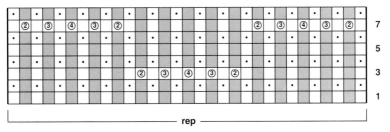

Note: On Rows 4 and 8, drop yos off needle.
On Rows 5 and 6, gently pull dropped yos into shape.

Cocoon

Multiple of 16 sts + 1.

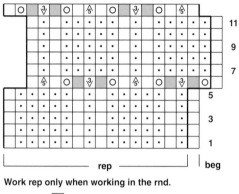

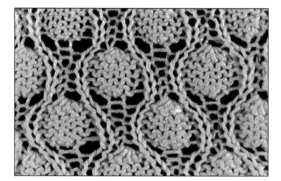

Work rep only when working in the rnd.

Note: work ⅜ as kf+b+f in rows, pf+b+f in rnds.
Work ⅕ as k5tog in rows, p5tog in rnds.

Os and Vs

In rows: *Multiple of 3 sts.*

Row 1: *K3tog, leave sts on left needle, knit into 1st st, knit next 2 sts tog through back loop, let all sts drop off; rep from *.

Row 2: Purl.

Rows 3 and 4: Knit.

Repeat Rows 1–4.

In rounds: *Multiple of 3 sts.*

Rnd 1: *K3tog, leave sts on left needle, knit into 1st st, knit next 2 sts tog through back loop, let all sts drop off; rep from *.

Rnds 2 and 3: Knit.

Rnd 4: Purl.

Repeat Rnds 1–4.

Shell

Multiple of 11 sts.
Note: M1: place a twisted loop over the right needle.

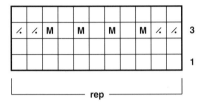

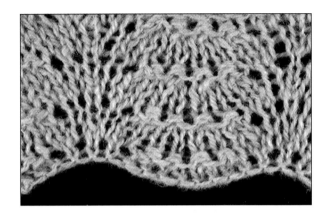

GEOMETRIC PATTERNS

Diamonds

In rows: *Multiple of 8 sts.*
Row 1: *P1, k7; rep from *.
Rows 2 and 8: *K1, p5, k1, p1; rep from *.
Rows 3 and 7: *K2, p1, k3, p1, k1; rep from *.
Rows 4 and 6: *P2, k1, p1, k1, p3; rep from *.
Row 5: *K4, p1, k3; rep from *.
Repeat Rows 1–8.

In rounds: *Multiple of 8 sts.*
Rnd 1: *P1, k7; rep from *.
Rnds 2 and 8: *K1, p1, k5, p1; rep from *.
Rnds 3 and 7: *K2, p1, k3, p1, k1; rep from *.
Rnds 4 and 6: *K3, p1, k1, p1, k2; rep from *.
Rnd 5: *K4, p1, k3; rep from *.
Repeat Rnds 1–8.

Basketweave

In rows: *Multiple of 6 sts.*
Rows 1 and 7: Knit.
Rows 2 and 8: Purl.
Rows 3 and 5: *K1, p4, k1; rep from *.
Rows 4 and 6: *P1, k4, p1; rep from *.
Rows 9 and 11: *P2, k2, p2; rep from *.
Rows 10 and 12: *K2, p2, k2; rep from *.
Repeat Rows 1–12.

In rounds: *Multiple of 6 sts.*
Rnds 1, 2, 7, and 8: Knit.
Rnds 3, 4, 5, and 6: *K1, p4, k1; rep from *.
Rnds 9, 10, 11, and 12: *P2, k2, p2; rep from *.
Repeat Rnds 1–12.

Piqué Squares

In rows: *Multiple of 12 sts.*
Rows 1, 3, and 5: *K6, [p2, with yarn in front sl 2 back to left needle, yarn back across 2 sts, return 2 sts to right needle] 3 times; rep from *.
Rows 2, 4, 6, 8, 10, and 12: Purl.
Rows 7, 9, and 11: *[P2, sl 2 back to left needle, yarn forward across 2 sts, return 2 sts to right needle] 3 times, k6; rep from *.
Repeat Rows 1–12.

In rounds: *Multiple of 12 sts.*
Rnds 1, 3, and 5: *K6, [p2, sl 2 back to left needle, yarn forward across 2 sts, return 2 sts to right needle] 3 times; rep from *.
Rnds 2, 4, 6, 8, 10, and 12: Knit.
Rnds 7, 9, and 11: *[P2, sl 2 back to left needle, yarn forward across 2 sts, return 2 sts to right needle] 3 times, k6; rep from *.
Repeat Rnds 1–12.

Bricks

In rows: *Multiple of 8 sts.*
Rows 1 and 3: *P6, k2; rep from *.
Rows 2 and 4: *P2, k6; rep from *.
Rows 5 and 7: *K2, p2, k4; rep from *.
Rows 6 and 8: *P4, k2, p2; rep from *.
Repeat Rows 1–8.

In rounds: *Multiple of 8 sts.*
Rnds 1, 2, 3, and 4: *P6, k2; rep from *.
Rnds 5, 6, 7, and 8: *K2, p2, k4; rep from *.
Repeat Rnds 1–8.

WAVY-STITCH PATTERNS FOR COLORBANDS AND BORDERS

Because of the heavy, two-layered effect of stranded colorwork, traditional shawls have never been knitted in the all-over color patterns of the Fair Isles sweaters, gloves, tams, and mufflers. However, bands of color have long been combined with wavy-edged openwork stitches to create lovely and exciting shawls. Such banded shawls were a particular favorite of the Shetland knitters.

Sarah Don reports in *The Art of Shetland Lace* (Bell and Hyman, 1981) that pastel-colored lace scarves in the wavy patterns remained popular on Shetland in the late 1970s and early 1980s, while red and white was previously the favored color scheme for knitted lace wedding veils. The recently popular combinations are most often white with rose-pink, blue, or dove-gray. Gray shawls with black and white borders, or dark brown with cream and beige have also been popular on Shetland. Once spun and dyed at home with local wool and vegetable dyes, traditional shawls and stoles are now also made with commercial yarns in a greater color range.

When working bands of color back and forth in rows (especially garter stitch or garter-based patterns), choose one side as the right side of the fabric, and always change to a new color on a right-side row. This will ensure that each band of color is uniform in appearance. When working in the round, every row is a right-side row, so there's no need for concern.

Working color changes will result in tail-ends of yarn that will need to be hidden. Instead of weaving them into the knitting with a blunt needle, try making the ends longer and knitting them together with the stitches on the needle. This will hide the ends quickly and easily.

Wavy-edged stitch patterns are often used for plain-knit, everyday shawls and hap scarves. In the Shetland Isles, these are usually plain garter stitch combined with openwork borders. Of all the wavy-edged patterns used for haps, Old Shale is certain-

ly the most common. The shale patterns are named for the way the waves look as they wash up upon a shale shoreline. Hap scarves and stoles are rather sturdily made in the same color combinations as shawls with colorbands. No edging is used—the wavy pattern itself creates the scallops along the cast-on or bind-off edges. New Shale, Cockleshell, or Chevron and Fagotting are the sort of stitches traditionally used and are still used for hap scarves today. To prevent the cast-on edge from looking different from the bind-off edge, some scarf makers knit two "ends" and graft them in the middle. Both ends are then cast-on edges and thus uniform in appearance.

SHELL/SHALE PATTERNS

Old Shale

Multiple of 12 sts.
Note: Row 4 can be knitted or purled, depending on whether or not you want a ridge of garter stitch. A garter ridge is often worked in old Shetland knitting, but other traditional knitters prefer to work this row in stockinette stitch.

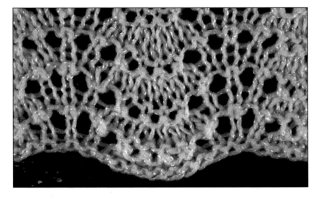

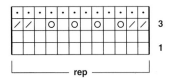

New Shale

Multiple of 10 sts + 7.

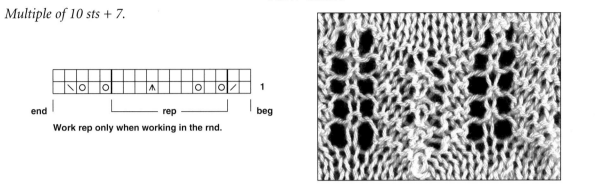

Work rep only when working in the rnd.

Cockleshell

Multiple of 19 sts.
Note: Double yarn-overs are used to make the open-
work more visible in the garter-based fabric.

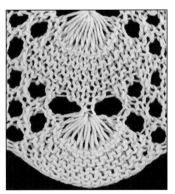

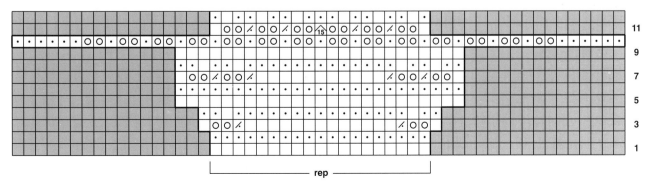

Shale Strand

Multiple of 11 sts + 2.

Note: The P2togs make a garter-stitch ridge on the right side of the knitting. If you prefer a smooth surface, substitute k2tog for each p2tog.

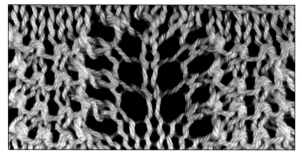

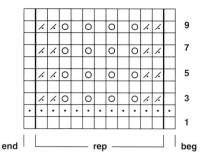

end | └── rep ──┘ | beg

Rows: Work edge st, rep bet heavy lines, work edge st.
Rnds: Delete edge sts; work bet heavy lines.

Feather

Multiple of 7 sts.

Note: The purl stitches in the first row make a line of garter across the pattern. You may eliminate this by substituting knit stitches for the purls.

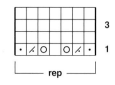

└── rep ──┘

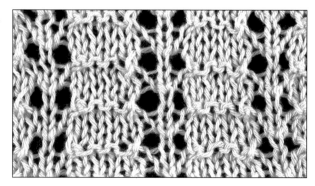

Pine Trees

Multiple of 12 sts + 1.

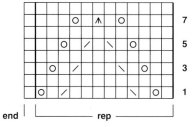

end | └── rep ──┘

Work rep only when working in the rnd.

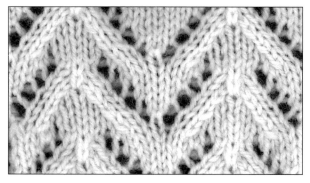

Fan Shell

Multiple of 15 sts + 4.

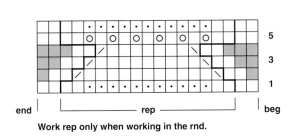

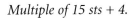

Work rep only when working in the rnd.

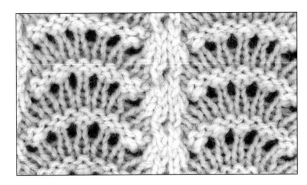

CHEVRON PATTERNS

Chevron Lace

Multiple of 6 sts + 2.

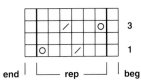

Work rep only when working in the rnd.

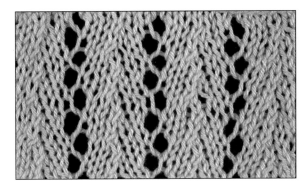

Chevron and Open Rib

Multiple of 9 sts + 2.

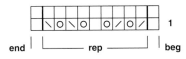

Work rep only when working in the rnd.

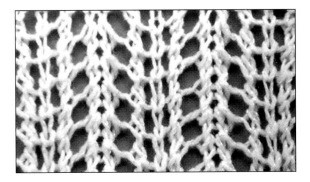

Gate and Ladder

Multiple of 9 + 12 sts.

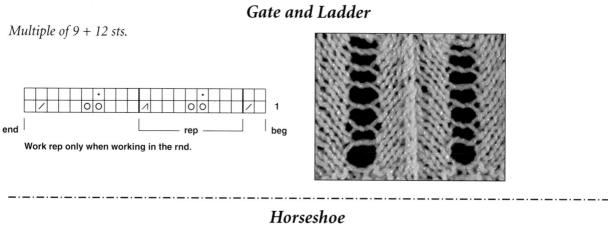

Work rep only when working in the rnd.

Horseshoe

Multiple of 10 sts + 2.

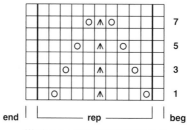

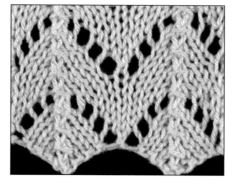

Work rep only when working in the rnd.

Razor Shell

Multiple of 8 sts + 1.

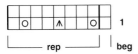

Work rep only when working in the rnd.

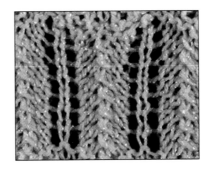

ALTERNATING MOTIFS

Fir Cone

Multiple of 10 sts + 11.
Note: End pattern with Row 8 or 16.

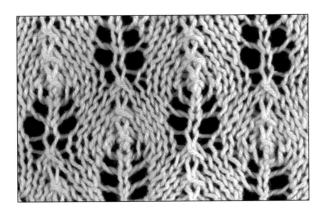

\			O		O			∧			O		O		/	15
\			O		O			∧			O		O		/	13
\			O		O			∧			O		O		/	11
\			O		O			∧			O		O		/	9
	O			∧			O		O			∧			O	7
	O			∧			O		O			∧			O	5
	O			∧			O		O			∧			O	3
	O			∧			O		O			∧			O	1

end | └─── rep ───┘ | beg

Work rep only when working in the rnd.

Ostrich Plumes

Multiple of 16 sts + 17.
Note: End pattern with Row 16 or 32.

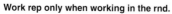

end | rep | beg

Work rep only when working in the rnd.

Crest of the Wave

Multiple of 12 sts + 1.

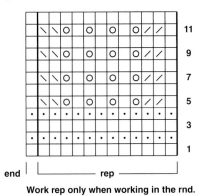

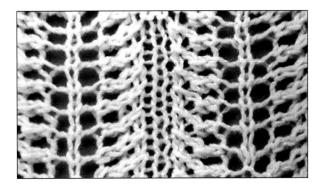

Work rep only when working in the rnd.

Openwork Leaf

Multiple of 8 sts + 9.

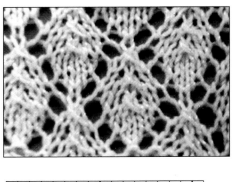

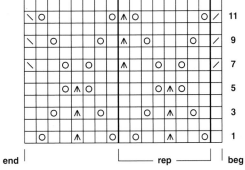

Work rep only when working in the rnd.

GARTER-BASED STITCH PATTERNS

These useful stitch patterns are openwork and textured with a background of garter stitch. Because it's so simple to knit and does not curl, garter stitch has long been prized by shawl knitters for shawls worked back and forth in rows. Traditionally, square shawl centers knitted on the bias (corner to corner) have been worked in garter stitch or a garter-based pattern. Garter-based patterns are also especially useful for triange, half-circle, and rectangle scarves and stoles.

Garter-based stitch patterns can be light and airy if the gauge is well chosen. Make sure your sample swatch has a stretchy, loose feel. If it feels a bit heavy or stiff, try larger needles. If you're accustomed to garter stitch as a very dense, tightly knit fabric, you'll be surprised by its appearance when worked with fine yarn and large needles. Because garter stitch is a stable fabric, it can hold its shape even when knitted quite loosely.

Just like stockinette-based patterns, openwork garter-based patterns are formed with combinations of yarn-overs and decreases. In some patterns, yarn-overs are worked in one row and decreases in the next. Some garter patterns, such as Cockleshell, use double yarn-overs. Just as the name implies, you wind the yarn twice over the needle. In the next row, this double yarn-over often becomes two stitches. Double yarn-overs make the openwork more visible in garter-textured fabrics. Triple and quadruple yarn-overs are used in some patterns, such as Seafoam, and require that the extra yarn loops be dropped for a special effect.

STRAIGHT-EDGED PATTERNS

Horizontal Lace Stitch

Multiple of 2 sts + 2.

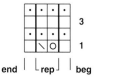

Work rep only when working in the rnd.

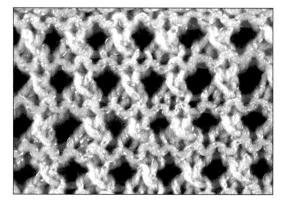

Garter Lace Stitch

Multiple of 8 sts + 2.

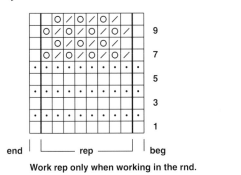

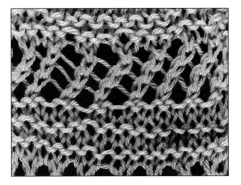

end   rep   beg

Work rep only when working in the rnd.

Garter Drop Stitch

Multiple of 2 sts + 2.

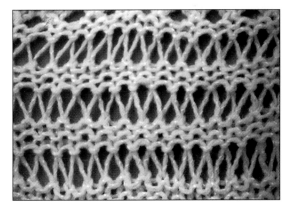

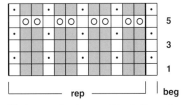

rep   beg

Work rep only when working in the rnd.

Lozenge Stitch

Multiple of 16 sts.
Note: End pattern with Row 12 or 24.

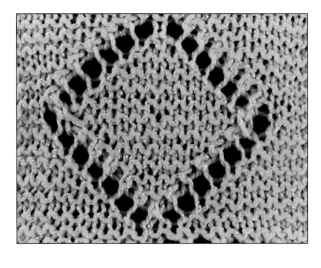

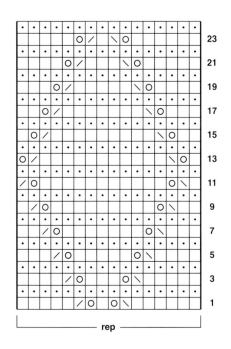

Crazy Check

Multiple of 16 sts + 2.

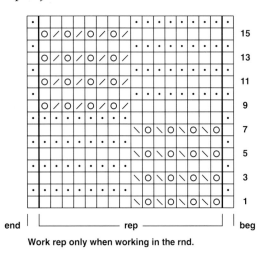

Work rep only when working in the rnd.

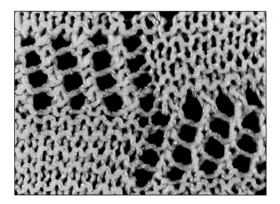

64

Van Dyke Madeira

Multiple of 8 sts.

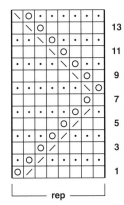

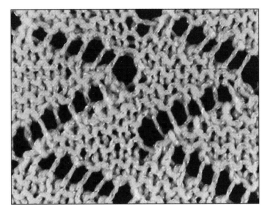

Madeira Mesh

Multiple of 6 sts + 7.

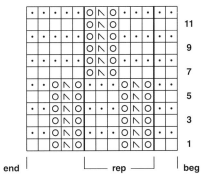

Work rep only when working in the rnd.

Note: Work 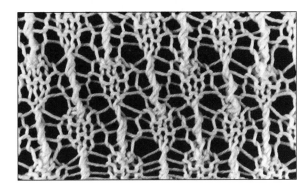 **as p3tog on both RS and WS rows.**

Tiles

Multiple of 12 sts.

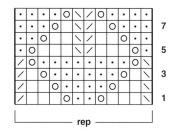

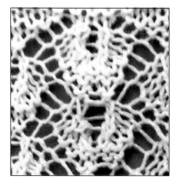

WAVY-EDGED PATTERNS

Tulips

Multiple of 13 sts.

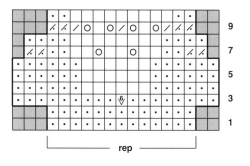

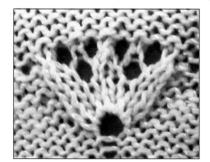

Aran Wheatears

Multiple of 12 sts + 1.

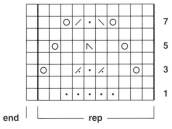

Work rep only when working in the rnd.

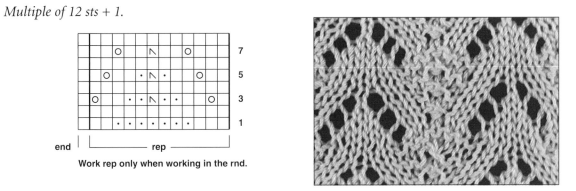

5 × 5 Wheatears

Multiple of 10 sts + 1.

Work rep only when working in the rnd.

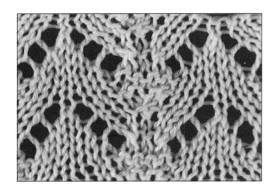

Fan Stitch or Lucina Shell

Multiple of 9 sts + 1.

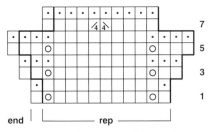

Work rep only when working in the rnd.

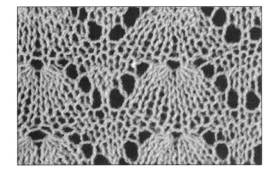

Madeira Leaf

Multiple of 12 sts + 17.

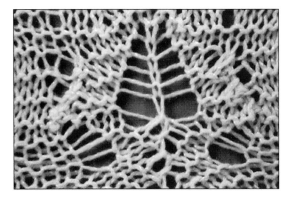

Work rep only when working in the rnd.

Note: Work ⋀ as p3tog on both RS and WS rows.

Work ⁄ as p2tog on both RS and WS rows.

SHAWL FINISHES

EDGES

Shawl edges must be as elastic as possible to allow for blocking (especially openwork designs) and to drape well. Nothing so spoils a shawl's appearance and feel as a tightly bound-off edge. If you bind off at all, it must be done very loosely.

Here are two ways of finishing a shawl that do not involve binding off and provide nice finishing touches. They are simple to do and make the shawl's edges elastic.

Fringed Edge

The very simplest finish is fringe. You may either hate it or love it, but it does finish a shawl simply and easily. Personal taste aside, the greatest disadvantage to fringe is that it uses up a surprisingly large amount of yarn. Its advantages are the simplicity of accomplishment, and the elasticity of edge it provides.

To apply fringe and "bind off" your edge in one fell swoop, simply cut several strands of yarn (more for thick fringe, less for thin) two times the length fringe you decide on; gather two, three, or four stitches from the left knitting needle onto a crochet hook, fold the fringe in half, catch it at the fold with the crochet hook, and pull the fold through the stitches on the crochet hook. Then feed the ends of the fringe through its folded loop and draw the loop closed over itself and the knit stitches. If the fringe is of a reasonable length (more than an inch when knotted), this simple knot will hold both stitches and fringe forever. Continue in this manner until all the shawl's stitches are off the needle.

Note: Don't gather up too many stitches in each fringe knot or you will lose the elasticity you need at the shawl's edge; depending on your yarn and gauge, sometimes even four stitches is too many.

To be precise about it, you can count up the total number of stitches to be "bound off", and make sure that the total is divisible by the number of stitches you are grouping together in each fringe knot. This way your stitches will come out even in the end. For example, if you have a total of 628 stitches, you can have either 2 or 4 stitches per fringe, and come out even at the end. On the other hand, if your edge has a total of 575 stitches, you will not come out even with either 2, 3, or 4 stitches per fringe. You can either gather up 5 stitches per fringe or space out the leftover 1 or 2 stitches where unobtrusive.

The best reason for dividing your total stitches by number of fringe knots before you start making the fringe is that you'll know how much fringe to cut. For example, if you have 628 stitches and you allow 4 stitches per fringe, you will need to cut 157 groups of fringe to knot all your stitches. If you like a thick fringe or a long fringe, you can see that it will take quite a bit of yarn, very often several skeins.

Crocheted-Off Edge

A quasi bind-off that I call the crocheted-off edge is worked much the same way as fringe. The crocheted-off edge makes for the fastest finishing and uses the least amount of yarn. It is also one of the prettiest edges, especially for a shawl with lots of openwork. Once again, the technique involves gathering several stitches together so you can divide them up evenly ahead of time, or beginning arbitrarily and dealing with the leftovers when and if they come up at the end.

Put the first two, three, or four stitches from your left needle onto a crochet hook, catch the supply yarn with the hook, and pull through the stitches on the hook. Chain five to ten (or more) stitches with the crochet hook (pull yarn through loop on hook), and take another set of stitches from the left needle onto the hook. Catch them with a single crochet stitch and make the same five to ten chain stitches again.

Repeat this procedure until all the stitches have been removed from the knitting needle and caught with a crochet stitch. Make one last chain, join it to the first clump of finished stitches, and knot off your yarn, weaving in the end. This very simple crochet technique can be modified by grouping more or fewer stitches together, by making a shorter or longer chain, or by working an entire crocheted

Crocheted-off edge.

edging onto the base of crochet chains. These crocheted chains can also be made very long and loopy, like a fringe.

Alternately, you can knot fringe onto each crocheted chain.

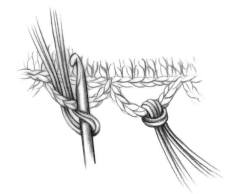

Fringe added with a crochet hook.

There are many possibilities for the crocheted-off shawl edge, but all are simple to do, and provide the stretchy edge a shawl needs.

Knitted-On Borders

A knitted-on border or edging is a more substantial finish than a crocheted-off edge. Border usually means a straight edge, while edging means an outer edge that's pointed, wavy, or shaped in some way.

A knitted-on border can be a very simple one of garter or seed stitch, or any other non-curling stitch pattern. It is accomplished by casting on the width of the border and knitting back and forth perpendicular to the shawl's edge, incorporating the border with the shawl edge stitch by stitch. The number of stitches you cast on will depend on how wide you want the border, and what pattern you are planning to knit. Garter or seed stitch can be knitted with any number of stitches, but other stitch patterns may

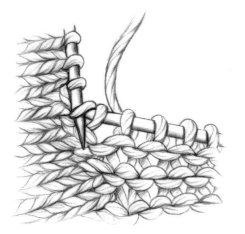

Garter-stitch border being knitted and attached to shawl-edge stitches with each right-side row.

require a specific number. If this technique is new to you, try a garter-stitch border first—knit every row—so you can concentrate on the technique.

If I have knitted a shawl in the round on a circular needle, I sometimes prefer to cap off my right needle-end and knit the border with the left needle and a short double-pointed needle—I put the second cap of the pair on the end of the double-pointed needle. Using an unattached right-hand needle prevents strain on the stitches between right and left ends of a circular needle—especially as you flip-flop the knitting to knit in back-and-forth rows. It also makes it easier to remember which row you're knitting, a knit or a purl, when you are knitting a fancy lace edging.

Plain Knitted-On Border Step-By-Step

1. For a straight-edged border, cast a reasonable number of stitches (usually between five and twenty) onto the left needle. Use a cable or a backward loop cast-on. This forms the only edge to be seamed later on.

2. Knit across these new stitches with the double-pointed needle. When you reach the last stitch, knit it together with the first stitch of your shawl edge. Now turn the work and knit the stitches off the double-pointed needle back onto the left of your circular needle. You'll finish this row back at the outer edge of the border. Continue in this manner, knitting back and forth, knitting the last border stitch together with the next shawl stitch every time you come to the shawl edge (every other row).

3. When you reach a corner (on a square, triangle, or rectangle), you must, of course, knit more rows per edge-of-shawl stitches than usual so that the border will lie flat as it turns the corner. If you make no alteration at the corner, the border may pull in unattractively at the outer edge, and the most severe blocking may not be able to flatten it. The wider your border is, the more extra rows you will need to keep the corner flat.

Think of race car drivers—they always try to round the corner of the track on the inside because the distance is shorter than on the outside. On plain, narrow borders (of about five to nine stitches) it is enough to add two extra pairs of rows (meaning knit across, knit back) at the very corner.

To add two extra pairs of rows:

1. Choose three stitches to represent the corner, one for the exact corner and a stitch on either side. Knit the border to the shawl edge as usual until you reach the first of the three corner stitches. Knit the border stitches toward the shawl edge, knitting the last border stitch together with the first corner stitch, turn, and then knit the border stitches out to the edge.

2. Now turn and knit toward the exact-corner stitch, but do not knit it together with the border—simply knit the last border stitch, turn, and then knit the border stitches out to the edge. This adds one extra pair of rows.

3. Knit again toward the corner stitch, and this time knit it together with the border, turn, and knit the border stitches out to the edge.

4. Knit again toward the corner stitch, but turn right after knitting the last stitch of the border and knit the border stitches out to the edge. This is the second pair of extra rows.

5. Finally, knit again toward the corner, and this time knit the border together with the third of the three corner stitches, turn, and knit the border stitches out to the edge.

Where stitches would normally have been knitted off in six rows of border, you have knitted ten rows of border to smoothly turn the corner.

For a wider border, knit more extra rows over three, four, five, six, or even seven corner stitches, in the same manner as above. If you are using four or six stitches as the corner stitches, the exact corner

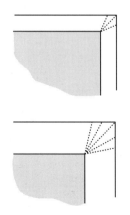

More rows added at corners for wider border.

will be in the space between two stitches. This is handy for some edging patterns made with an even number of stitches. When you have knit off the last shawl-edge stitches, bind off the border, and seam the cast-on and bind-off edges together, weaving in all the ends of yarn. That's it! You have a beautifully elastic border that will stretch with the shawl.

Lace Edging

To knit a lace edging for a border, choose an edging pattern that is not too wide (between five and twenty stitches), and read through it carefully. You must determine which edge is the straight, flat edge meant to go against the shawl edge, and which is the pointed or wavy edge, meant to go on the outside. Most patterns repeat after four, six, eight, ten, or twelve rows; the eight-row pattern is probably the most common.

As you are reading through an edging pattern, the rows which always have the same starting sequence will usually be the flat, inner edge. For example, "Sl 1, k1, p2tog" is a very common start for the inner edge. If a slipped stitch is the first stitch in a row, you can usually assume that it is meant to be a nice, firm selvedge edge. For the knitted-on border, you can simply knit such slipped stitches since you're joining the border to the shawl, and have no straight selvedge edge to contend with.

The outer side of an edging can often be spotted in the instruction to "bind off X number of stitches" in or near the last row of the pattern. This binding off forms the pointed side of many edgings.

Very often the first row of an edging pattern goes outward, toward the wavy edge, which is exactly what you want. Odd rows go outward, while even rows go inward toward the shawl edge. If an edging does not start with an outward-moving row, you

Knitted lace edging curves around corners when additional rows are added.

Cast-on and bind-off edges are seamed together at the fourth corner.

may be able to add a new first row, or shift the old one to the end of the pattern and start with Row 2.

Edgings almost always have some "activity" in every row, unlike other lace patterns which simply purl back on alternate rows. This means that lace edgings often have a mixture of knit and purl on both sides of the work; this feature prevents the edging from curling and makes it look nice on both sides.

As with plain borders, lace edgings must have extra rows to help them go around corners and still lie flat. The wider the edging, the more extra rows you must add at the corners. The extra rows can be spaced evenly over several stitches, as with a plain border, but remember that you must stay in pattern as you work. The "extra" rows must be rows of the pattern you're using, but they are spaced over fewer stitches. For example, if your edging pattern is eight rows long on the flat side, those eight rows "consume" four stitches of your shawl edge. When you reach the corner, make those same eight rows consume only two stitches of the shawl edge.

Edgings do take time to knit on, but their beauty, elasticity, and lightness make them well worth the effort—and you are binding off at the same time! If you discover that you enjoy knitting an edging, try it on its own as well. In a light cotton crochet thread it may make a beautiful lace trimming for linens.

After your shawl is bordered and finished, but before you block it, take time to darn in any loose

Darn in loose ends.

ends of yarn. Thread the yarn onto a blunt-tipped tapestry needle (I like the large plastic ones), and run it through the knitted fabric as inconspicuously as you can. To prevent the end from pulling out, reverse the direction you're weaving in at least once. If your end is a bit short, weave the needle through the fabric first, starting close by the short end; then, with the needle in the fabric, thread the yarn end through the eye, and pull the needle out. The short end will disappear.

Do not cut off any yarn-ends short at the knot; knots have a way of slyly unknotting when there is no end to hold them in place. If you are using singles wool, it is especially important to weave the loose ends in: single-ply wool ends can easily untwist, fray, and eventually disintegrate. Just a little extra time and care on your part may add years to the life of your shawl.

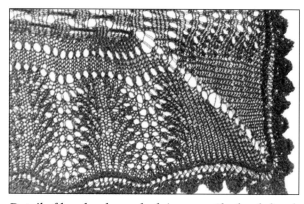

Detail of lace border and edging on a Shetland shawl.

LACE EDGING PATTERNS

Stripes and Points

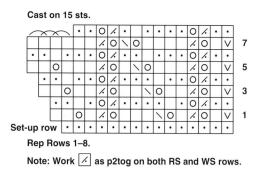

Cast on 15 sts.

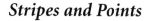

Rep Rows 1–8.

Note: Work ⟋ as p2tog on both RS and WS rows.

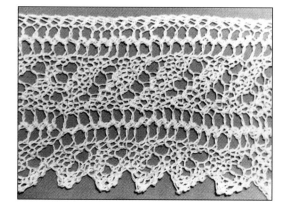

Narrow Points

Cast on 6 sts.

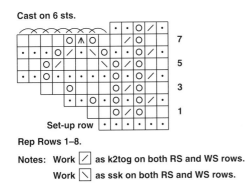

Rep Rows 1–8.

Notes: Work ╱ as k2tog on both RS and WS rows.

　　　 Work ╲ as ssk on both RS and WS rows.

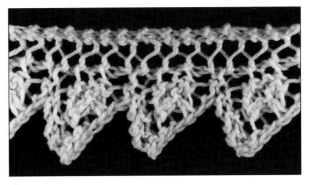

Stripe and Loops

Cast on 11 sts.

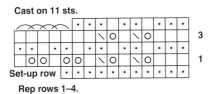

Rep rows 1–4.

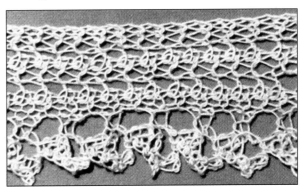

Ocean Waves

Cast on 13 sts.

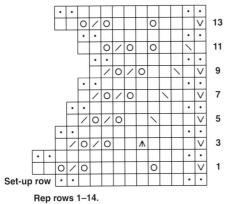

Rep rows 1–14.

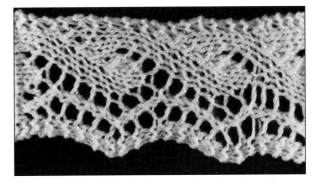

Narrow Van Dyke

Cast on 7 sts.

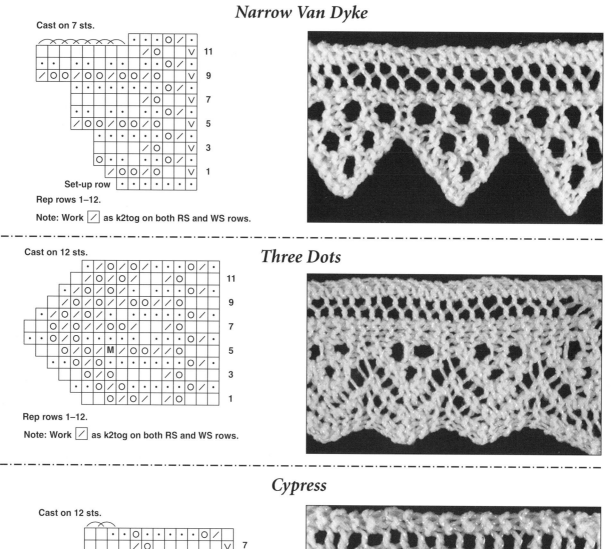

Rep rows 1–12.

Note: Work ◻ as k2tog on both RS and WS rows.

Three Dots

Cast on 12 sts.

Rep rows 1–12.

Note: Work ◻ as k2tog on both RS and WS rows.

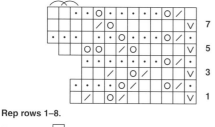

Cypress

Cast on 12 sts.

Rep rows 1–8.

Note: Work ◻ as k2tog on both RS and WS rows.

Smallest Points

Cast on 5 sts.

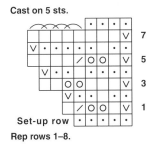

Rep rows 1–8.

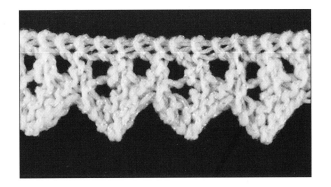

Leaf

Cast on 8 sts.

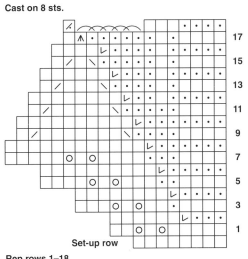

Rep rows 1–18.

Cast on 14 sts.

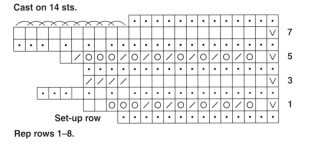

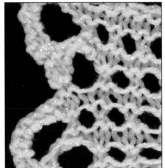

Rep rows 1–8.

Cast on 10 sts.

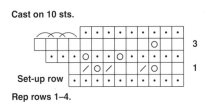

Rep rows 1–4.

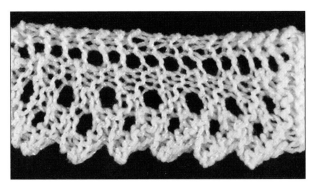

Note: This edging is rather fluted and works especially well around the perimeter of a circular or half-circular shawl.

Caring for Shawls

Finishing

Because of the soft, flexible nature of a knitted shawl, blocking is an important part of its finishing and maintenance. Blocking is the controlled stretching, shaping, and straightening of a damp knitted piece to produce a desired size and shape. Openwork patterns demand the most serious stretching, while other stitch patterns may require only minor adjustment and shaping of the edges. Blocking can cause a dramatic change in the size of a shawl. Some pieces can be blocked only slightly to form smaller, denser, warmer shawls, or dramatically stretched into giant, gauzy, lightweight shawls. And because a shawl must be blocked after every washing, you can change its shape every time you wash it. Once dry, however, a shawl retains the blocked shape until it is wetted again.

Not all fibers react in the same way to the blocking process. Some synthetic "memory" yarns will not stretch and cannot be blocked in any way. Wool stretches more than other natural fibers, but all natural fibers benefit from the evening-out effects of blocking.

Blocking may (though it need not) include washing, but either way, the shawl must be thoroughly dampened before blocking. If you choose to wash the shawl first, follow the steps below for excellent results.

Washing

1. Fill a basin with lukewarm water. Very hot water will cause shrinking; cold water is too shocking to fibers and your hands. Add a mild soap intended for hand-washing and work it up into a lather.

2. Place the shawl in the water and gently squeeze the suds through the fibers. Let the shawl soak ten to twenty minutes, or longer if it is very dusty or stained.

3. Lift the shawl out of the water, supporting its full weight with your hands so that it doesn't stretch. Gently squeeze out some excess water while supporting it—do not wring it. Set the shawl aside (in a dishpan, on the other side of a double sink, etc.). Drain the basin.

4. Rinse the shawl three times in this way, taking care to remove the shawl from the basin each time you add water (allowing water to pour over wool may cause felting). If you like, add a little fabric softener to the final rinse (before adding the shawl). Wool's texture may benefit from a fabric softener, though it can stain silk.

5. If possible, place the shawl in a washing machine, evenly distributing its weight in the basket and adding a heavy towel for balance if necessary. Turn the machine on the spin cycle and spin at top speed—the more water you can remove at this point, the faster the shawl will dry and the less chance it will pull out of shape. Immediately remove the shawl from the machine and shake it gently a few times to fluff it up. It should be damp-dry.

Blocking

In Scotland lace knitters used specially-made frames to block lace shawls or they "pegged them out" on grassy knolls. Alternatively, you can use a towel-covered queen- or king-sized bed or a large patch of carpeted floor.

Begin by stretching the shawl evenly in four directions for squares, rectangles, and circles, and in three directions for triangles and half circles. Pin the edges in place with T-pins or quilter's pins.

Work your way around the edges, alternating from side to side, stretching and pinning until the whole outer edge of the shawl is pinned. Slant the pins outward so the edge of the shawl doesn't pop off. Measure from the center of the shawl out to each edge to ensure that you have stretched the shawl evenly. Also measure the sides of squares and triangles to make sure they are of equal lengths. Some shawl designs (such as openwork) will require more stretching than others. Judge for yourself as you go how much to stretch.

Leave the shawl pinned out until it is completely dry. You can speed the process by setting a fan to blow across it. A wool shawl that has been spun damp-dry will completely dry in half a day or less; most shawls will certainly dry overnight. However, if you peg out a shawl on the lawn (see page 114), beware of dew (it will increase drying time), and of course, avoid strong sunlight on wool.

See page 114 for other ways to block shawls.

STORING

When you don't use a shawl regularly, wash it, block it, fold it, and place it in a safe place away from sunlight, moths, crickets, mice, dampness, and any other fiber-destroyer. Wool and silk are especially prone to such damage. Don't risk finding your careful handwork full of holes that you did not knit into it.

A strongly-scented cedar chest is ideal for safe storage. Renew the scent of an old chest by sanding the cedar. Another safeguard is to store strong-smelling herbal sachets or mothballs along with your shawls. Periodically check to make sure that

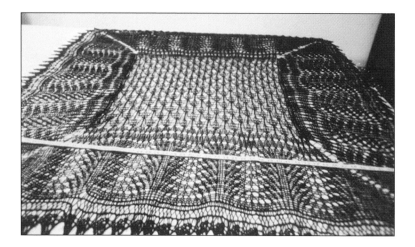

Shawl pinned into position to dry.

these maintain their scent; only a strong scent will discourage moths. A particularly good moth repellent is Yardley's English Lavender Soap—it has a pleasant scent that lasts for a long time and it is non-toxic. (For maximum effectiveness, be sure to remove the soap from the box.)

MENDING

Pulled threads or snags can usually be worked back into the fabric by stretching the area of knitting around the snagged stitch. A dropped stitch can be secured by tying a loop of the same yarn (you did save some, didn't you?) through the dropped stitch and the stitch above or beside it, and then weaving in the ends. If you don't have some of the same yarn, you can use matching sewing thread.

If the yarn breaks and causes a hole, mend it immediately. Tie new yarn to one end of the broken stitch, graft a new stitch or two using a blunt-end needle, and tie the new end to the other broken end. Then weave in the loose ends. Use sewing thread and needle, if that's all you have, or take the shawl to an expert for mending, but do mend it!

Given good yarn, good workmanship, and good care, a knitted shawl can outlive its knitter, providing warmth and pleasure to several generations of family and friends.

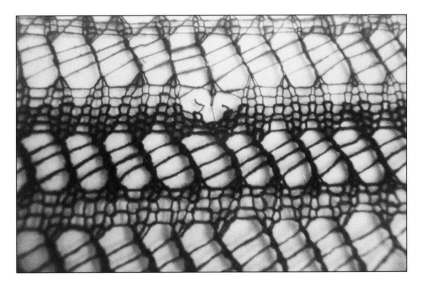

Hole to be mended.

WEARING SHAWLS WITH STYLE

STYLES AND DRAPES

When all the work is done, the greatest pleasure of handknitted shawls is yet to come: wearing them. There are several ways to drape shawls. But first let's consider style.

In general, the finer the fabric, the dressier the shawl. Light yarn, lacy openwork, and a fancy finish make the most formal shawls, especially in white, cream, or black—the traditional colors of real lace. They look classic any time of the year. Mohair yarns also look rich and dressy for winter wear. Silk can be worn year round, while wool works for all but the hottest days of summer. Solid colors look more formal, as does smooth yarn. Slubbed yarns offer visual interest and a casual "arty" appearance. Also casual are flecked or tweedy yarns, two or more colors, and heavy yarns. Dark colors seem cooler, more classic, while "hot" colors demand attention. In the final analysis, shawl fabric is very much like clothing fabric.

Your own style is an important factor when fitting shawls into your wardrobe. If you are a tailored, no-frills kind of person, a shawl with fringes and flounces may not suit you. On the other hand, a simple mohair stole in a gorgeous color will add personality to your tailored winter suits. If you are ultra-modern, try classic white or black lace with a plain finish. For a sporty look, make a scarf-size triangle to wear over your shoulders. If you are knitting for someone else, be sure to consider their individual style.

Shawls for men? Sure, why not? I was delighted a few years ago to see Sherlock Holmes (on Public TV's *Mystery*) sporting a variety of knitted mufflers and even, on one occasion, a shawl. Of course, Sherlock Holmes was a bit eccentric, but if you are a male knitter, you aren't the sort to let that stand in your way! Capes, cloaks, and simple fabric wraps were once unisex apparel, and the way men handled fabric in former times is part of what was called "swashbuckling". It's still "way cool".

Knowing several ways to drape and wear a shawl will help you incorporate them into your wardrobe and wear them with panache. One of the first problems to overcome is a shawl sliding off your shoulders. One way to solve this is to wear a garment with a little texture under the shawl. And quite a few shawl drapes offer stability as well as style.

The simple drape is made by folding a square or circle in half along the diagonal. Or use a triangle or half circle. With the shawl centered on your shoulders and the points draped over each arm, pin the two ends behind your back and let the shawl's tail cover them. If the shawl fabric is delicate, support it by pinning the ends at your waist. If the shawl slips off your shoulders, pin it to your collar at the nape of the neck, unobtrusively, or use a brooch to secure one shoulder to your top or jacket.

The Spanish drape works well with a large, lightweight shawl. A folded square or circle or a large tri-

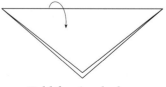

Fold for simple drape.

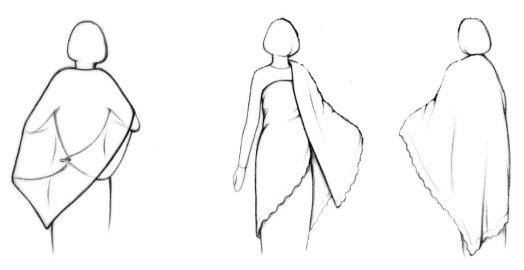

Simple drape.   *Spanish drape, front view.*   *Spanish drape, back view.*

angle or half circle all serve. One end wraps from the armpit across the back and around the chest, while the other end goes over the shoulder, sari-like. You can secure the wrapped side with a pin. The shawl itself is the focus of this drape, so it must be beautiful and not upstaged by what you wear under it.

The evening wrap drape is ideal for wearing over an evening ensemble or a coat. Any shawl shape will work. Center the shawl at the nape of the neck (and pin it there, if you wish), and pin the two points to the side of the shawl creating armhole openings. You can also pin two corners of a rectangle together around the wrist for the same armhole effect.

The scarf drape is exactly what you'd think—like an opera or aviator's silk scarf, the shawl is simply worn around the neck with the ends hanging down in front. Use a rectangle or a square folded into a rectangle. A triangle with the point folded under can work too.

The short revers drape can be used with a square, circle, or wide rectangle folded in uneven halves or

Evening wrap drape.

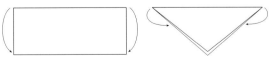

Fold for evening wrap drape.

STEP-BY-STEP INSTRUCTIONS

GATE AND LADDER CIRCLE SHAWL
Worked in rounds

This simple-to-knit shawl has a very open pattern. It is worked with a double yarn-over that is caught up securely in the following round. Because this pattern requires blocking for the lacy pattern to show well, use a yarn that blocks well.

Like many other wavy-edged patterns, Gate and Ladder looks nice when knit in colorbands. For a traditional look, use several shades of a neutral color, such as gray or oatmeal. Or work the shawl in black with bold stripes of red, green, and gold. A color scheme favored in Britain is one or more pastel shades combined with white or cream.

This shawl, worked from the center outward, is begun with just two needles and garter stitch. Although this old-fashioned pattern calls for k3tog double decreases, you could substitute the more commonly used sl 2 kwise, k1, p2sso decrease instead.

The shawl pictured was worked with 10 ounces of 3-ply sport-weight alpaca on size 6 (4 mm) needles. It is bordered with twenty-four rounds of Alternating Feathers. The finished diameter is 48" (122 cm).

Note: The Gate and Ladder pattern is wavy and will make the outer edge undulate. For a straight edge, end the shawl with twelve or more rounds of plain knitting or a straight-edged stitch pattern. Some other openwork patterns that fit evenly into 576 sts are St. John's Wort, Van Dyke and Rib, and Dew Drop.

Leaving a 6" tail, cast on 9 sts onto
   a dpn.
Row 1: Knit.
Row 2: K1 f&b in each st—18 sts.
Row 3: Knit. Divide sts evenly on 3
   or 4 dpn. Place m and join,
   being careful not to twist sts.
Rnds 4 and 5: Knit.
Rnd 6: *K1, yo; rep from *—36 sts.
Rnds 7–12: Knit.
Rnd 13: *K1, yo; rep from *—72
   sts.
Rnd 14: Knit.

Begin Gate and Ladder pattern:
Rnds 15, 17, 19, 21, and 23: *K3, yo
   twice, k3, k3tog; rep from *.
Rnds 16, 18, 20, 22, and 24: Knit,

except k1 f&b in each "yo twice".

Rnd 25: *K1, yo; rep from *—144 sts.

Rnd 26: Knit.

Rnds 27–38: Rep Rnds 15 and 16 six times.

Rnd 39: Rep Rnd 25—288 sts.

Rnd 40: Knit.

Rnds 41–64: Rep Rnds 15 and 16 twelve times.

Rnd 65: Rep Rnd 25—576 sts.

Rnd 66: Knit.

Rnds 67 and 68: Rep Rnds 15 and 16.

Alternate these last 2 rnds for as many more reps as desired, up to a total of 158 rnds (inc after every st on the 159th rnd). Most shawls are large enough after a total of 86 to 106 rnds.

Next-to-last Rnd: Knit.

Last Rnd: Crochet off, or knit on a border or edging.

Finishing: Use cast-on tail to sew tog edges along first few rows of knitting at the center of the shawl. Block. Add fringe if desired.

OS AND VS CIRCLE SHAWL
Worked in rays

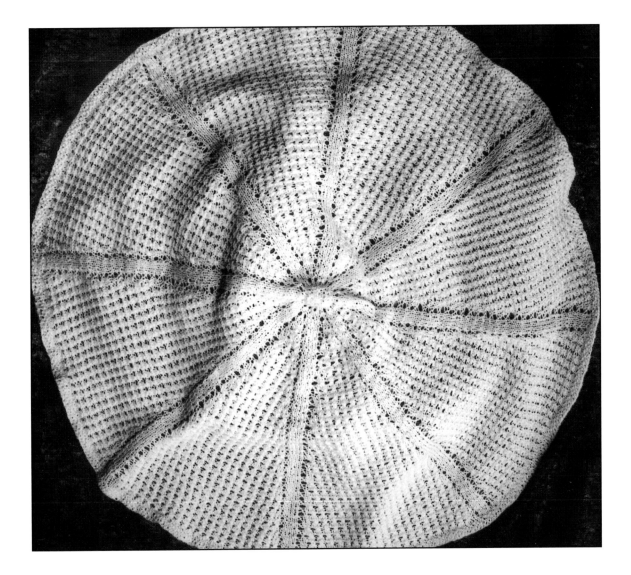

This shawl is worked from the center outward with lines of increase along rays worked in stockinette stitch, making them look much like the spokes of a wheel against the patterned background. The advantage of the rays method of increase is that it lies perfectly flat without blocking. Therefore, this shawl can be made with unblockable synthetic yarn.

The Os and Vs pattern forms twisted stitches, similar to a cable stitch. But because the stitches always remain on the needle, no cable needle is needed. To facilitate knitting three stitches together on the pattern rounds, take care to purl the pattern stitches loosely on the preceeding rounds.

The shawl pictured was worked with 8 ounces of 4-ply fingering weight wool/nylon blend (75% wool, 25% nylon) on size 5 (3.75 mm) needles. It is bordered with 4 rows of seed stitch and has a finished diameter of 34" (86.5 cm).

Cluster: (worked over 3 sts)
*k3tog, but leave sts on left needle, then knit the first st again and k2tog tbl; rep from *.

Lace Pattern: (beg with 72 sts)
Rnd 1: (RS) *K2, yo, k1, work Cluster to 3 sts before m, k1, yo, k2; rep from *—16 sts inc'd.
Rnds 2 and 3: Knit.
Rnd 4: *K4, purl to 4 sts before m, k4; rep from *.
Rnd 5: *K2, yo, k2, work Cluster to 4 sts before m, k2, yo, k2; rep from *—16 sts inc'd.
Rnds 6 and 7: Knit.
Rnd 8: *K5, purl to 5 sts before m, k5; rep from *.
Rnd 9: *K2, yo, work Cluster to 2 sts before m, yo, k2; rep from *—16 sts inc'd.
Rnds 10 and 11: Knit.
Rnd 12: *K3, purl to 3 sts before m, k3; rep from *.
Rep Rnds 1–12 for pattern.
Cast on 6 sts onto a dpn, leaving a 6" tail of yarn for seaming later.
Row 1: (WS) Knit.
Row 2: (RS) K1 f&b in each st— 12 sts.
Rows 3, 4, and 5: Knit.
Row 6: Rep Row 2—24 sts.

Divide sts evenly on 3 or 4 dpn and divide into 8 sections by placing a marker after every 3 sts to mark lines of increase—8 markers total (use a different colored marker at beg of rnd). Join into a circle, being careful not to twist sts. (Work rem shawl in the rnd.) Knit 3 rnds. *[K1, yo] 2 times, k1; rep from *—40 sts. Knit 3 rnds. *K2, yo, k1, yo, k2; rep from *—56 sts. Knit 3 rnds. *K2, yo, k3, yo, k2; rep from *— 72 sts. Knit 3 rnds. Work Lace patt, inc 2 sts each section (16 incs total) every 4 rnds until piece is desired size, ending with Rnd 4, 8, or 12 of patt. Crochet off all sts or work several rounds of ribbing (1 x 1, 2 x 2, or one given below) and then crochet off or bind off the sts very loosely. Using a tapestry needle, use the cast-on tail to sew the edges of the first rows of knitting. Weave in loose ends. Block.

Moss Knit Rib: Multiple of 4 sts
Rnd 1: *K3, p1, rep from *.
Rnd 2: K1, *p1, k3; rep from *, ending last rep k2.
Rep Rnds 1 and 2 for pattern.

Dot and Rib: Multiple of 2 sts
Rnd 1: *K1, p1; rep from *.
Rnd 2: Knit.
Rep Rnds 1 and 2 for pattern.

FAN STITCH HALF-CIRCLE SHAWL
In rounds on garter-stitch background

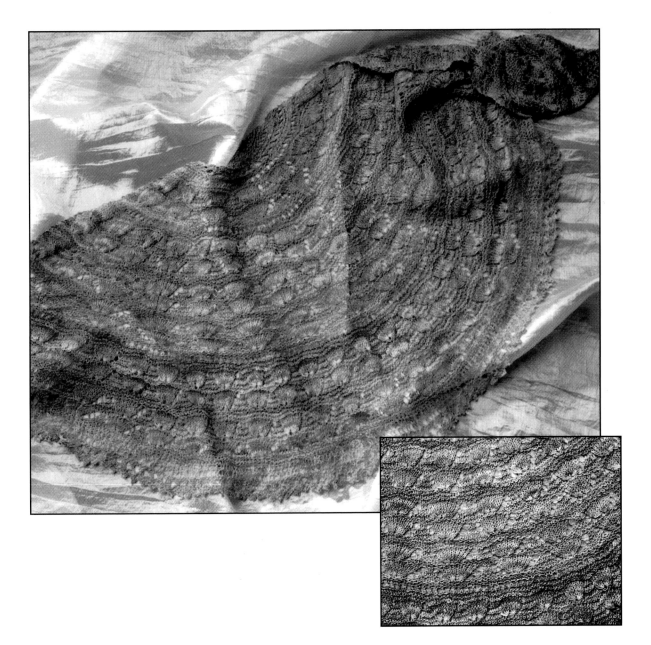

Half-circle shawls of the "rounds" increase method are hypnotic to knit because there are so many plain rows between the shaping increases. Because this shawl's shaping is not dependent on its final size, you can knit it in just about any yarn with just about any needle. If you use a blockable yarn, you can make the half-circle lie flat. If your yarn is not blockable, there will be a ruffle effect after the increase rounds, especially the last one, but this is pleasant-looking, too. Stop knitting whenever you feel you have reached the size you want, ending with 4 rows of garter stitch. (See page 28 for ideas on determining the ideal size.)

The shawl pictured was worked with 2-ply hand-dyed, handspun Pima cotton on size 3 (3.25 mm) needles. It has a finished diameter of 58" (147.5 cm). Shawl courtesy of Lynn Williams.

Cast on 5 sts. Knit 1 row.

Row 1: (RS) Knit in front and back of every stitch—10 sts.

Rows 2–4: Knit.

Row 5: *K1, yo; rep from * to last st, knit in front and back of last st—20 sts.

Rows 6–10: Knit.

Row 11: Rep Row 5—40 sts.

Rows 12–16: Knit.

Row 17: K1, *yo, k2tog; rep from * to last st, k1.

Rows 18–23: Knit.

Row 24: Rep Row 5—80 sts.

Rows 25–27: Knit.

Row 28: Knit into front and back of first st, k78, knit into front and back of last st—82 sts.

Row 29: *K2, yo, k8, yo; rep from *, end k2.

Row 30: K3, *p8, k4; rep from *, end last rep k3.

Row 31: K3, *yo, k8, yo, k4; rep from *, end last rep k3.

Row 32: K4, *p8, k6; rep from *, end last rep k4.

Row 33: K4, *yo, k8, yo, k6; rep from *, end last rep k4.

Row 34: K5, *p8, k8; rep from *, end last rep k5.

Row 35: K5, *k4tog tbl, k4tog, k8; rep from *, end last rep k5.

Row 36: Knit.

Rows 37–44: Rep Rows 29–36.

Rows 45–48: Knit.

Row 49: *K1, yo; rep from * to last 2 sts, k2—162 sts.

Rows 50–54: Knit.

Rows 55–114: Rep Rows 29–48 three times.

Rows 115–120: Rep Rows 49–54—322 sts.

Rows 121–160: Rep Rows 29–48 two times.

Bind off with a crocheted-off edge or work a knitted-on border (see page 70). If needed, stabilize the selvedge (top) edge by working a knitted-on or crocheted narrow border, picking up stitches along the selvedge edge. Block if needed.

COCOON STITCH HALF-CIRCLE SHAWL
Worked in rays

In this half-circle, the four ever-widening "rays" of Cocoon stitch are bordered by three stitches of garter stitch. Yarn-over increases are made at the edges of each ray. These are the rows that begin "K3, yo" once the stitch pattern has been established. Cocoon stitch looks fine on both sides of the fabric,

so it is a good choice for a half-circle or triangle.

The shawl pictured was worked with 5 ounces of a light sport-weight, washable wool blend (75% wool, 25% polyamid). It was worked at an unblocked garter-stitch gauge of 5 ½ stitches per inch and has a finished length of 28" (71 cm).

Cast on 5 sts.

Row 1: (WS) Knit.

Row 2: (K1, p1, k1) in each st—15 sts.

Rows 3, 4, and 5: Knit.

Row 6: *K3, yo twice; rep from *, end k3—23 sts.

Row 7: *K3, (k1, p1) in each "yo twice"; rep from *, end k3.

Rows 8 and 9: Knit.

Row 10: *K3, yo, k2, yo; rep from *, end k3—31 sts.

Rows 11, 12, and 13: Knit.

Row 14: *K3, yo, k4, yo; rep from *, end k3—39 sts.

Rows 15, 16, and 17: Knit.

Row 18: *K3, yo, k6, yo; rep from *, end k3—47 sts.

Rows 19, 20, and 21: Knit.

Row 22: *K3, yo, k1, p2, p2tog, p2, k1, yo; rep from *, end k3—51 sts.

Row 23: K4, *p1, k5; rep from *, end last rep k4.

Row 24: K5, *p5, k7; rep from *, end last rep k5.

Row 25: K4, *p1, k5; rep from *, end last rep k4.

Row 26: *K3, yo, p1, k1, p5, k1, p1, yo; rep from *, end k3—59 sts.

Row 27: *K3, p1, k1, p1, k5, p1, k1, p1; rep from *, end k3.

Row 28: K4, *p1, k1, p5, k1, p1, k5; rep from *, end last rep k4.

Row 29: K3, *p1, yo, (k1, p1, k1) in next st, yo, p1, p5tog, p1, yo, (k1, p1, k1) in next st, yo, p1, k3; rep from *—75 sts.

Row 30: *K3, yo, k1, p5, k1, p1, k1, p5, k1, yo; rep from *, end k3—83 sts.

Row 31: K4, *p1, k5, p1, k1, p1, k5, p1, k5; rep from *, end last rep k4.

Row 32: *K3, p1, k1, p5, k1, p1, k1, p5, k1, p1; rep from *, end k3.

Row 33: K4, *p1, k5, p1, k1, p1, k5, p1, k5; rep from *, end last rep k4.

Row 34: *K3, yo, p1, k1, p5, k1, p1, k1, p5, k1, p1, yo; rep from *, end k3—91 sts.

Row 35: *K3, [p1, yo, (k1, p1, k1) in next st, yo, p1, p5tog] 2 times, p1, yo, (k1, p1, k1) in next st, yo, p1; rep from *, end k3—107 sts.

Row 36: K4, *[p5, k1, p1, k1] 2 times, p5, k5; rep from *, end k4.

Row 37: *K3, p1, [k5, p1, k1, p1] 2 times, k5, p1; rep from *, end k3.

Row 38: *K3, yo, k1, [p5, k1, p1, k1] 2 times, p5, k1, yo; rep from *, end k3—115 sts.

Row 39: K4, *p1, [k5, p1, k1, p1] 2 times, k5, p1, k5; rep from *, end last rep k4.

Row 40: *K3, p1, k1, [p5, k1, p1, k1] 2 times, p5, k1, p1; rep from *, end k3.

Row 41: K4, *p1, [p5tog, p1, yo, (k1, p1, k1) in next st, yo, p1] 2 times, p5tog, p1, k5; rep from *, end last rep k4—99 sts.

Row 42: *K3, yo, p1, [k1, p1, k1, p5] 2 times, [k1, p1] 2 times, yo; rep from *, end k3—107 sts.

Row 43: K5, *[p1, k1, p1, k5] 2 times, p1, k1, p1, k7; rep from *, end last rep k5.

Row 44: K4, *p1, [k1, p1, k1, p5] 2 times, [k1, p1] 2 times, k5; rep from *, end last rep k4.

Row 45: *K3, p1, k1, [p1, k1, p1, k5] 2 times, [p1, k1] 2 times, p1; rep from *, end k3.

Row 46: *K3, yo, k1, p1, [k1, p1, k1, p5] 2 times, [k1, p1] 2 times, k1, yo; rep from *, end k3—115 sts.

Row 47: K4, *p1, k1, [p1, yo, (k1, p1, k1) in next st, yo, p1, p5tog] 2 times, p1, yo, (k1, p1, k1) in next st, yo, p1, k1, p1, k5; rep from *, end last rep k4—131 sts.

Row 48: *K3, p1, [k1, p1, k1, p5] 3 times, [k1, p1] 2 times; rep from *, end k3.

Row 49: K4, *[p1, k1, p1, k5] 3 times, p1, k1, p1, k5; rep from *, end last rep k4.

Row 50: *K3, yo, p1, [k1, p1, k1, p5] 3 times, [k1, p1] 2 times, yo; rep from *, end k3—139 sts.

Row 51: K5, *p1, k1, p1, [k5, p1, k1, p1] 3 times, k7; rep from *, end last rep k5.

Row 52: *K3, p2, k1, p1, k1, [p5, k1, p1, k1] 3 times, p2,; rep from *, end k3.

Row 53: K5, *[p1, yo, (k1, p1, k1) in next st, yo, p1, p5tog] 3 times, p1, yo, (k1, p1, k1) in next st, yo, p1, k7; rep from *, end k5—155 sts.

Row 54: *K3, yo, k1, p1, k1, [p5, k1, p1, k1] 4 times, yo; rep from *, end k3—163 sts.

Row 55: K4, *p1, k1, p1, [k5, p1, k1, p1] 4 times, k5; rep from *, end last rep k4.

Row 56: K3, p1, *k1, p1, k1, [p5, k1, p1, k1] 4 times, k5; rep from *, end p1, k3.

Row 57: K4, *p1, k1, p1, [k5, p1, k1, p1] 4 times, k5; rep from *, end last rep k4.

Row 58: *K3, yo, [p1, k1] 2 times, [p5, k1, p1, k1] 4 times, p1, yo; rep from *, end k3—171 sts.

Row 59: K5, *[p1, yo, (k1, p1, k1) in next st, yo, p1, p5tog] 4 times, p1, yo, (k1, p1, k1) in next st, yo, p1, k7; rep from *, end last rep k5—187 sts.

Row 60: K4, *p1, k1, [p5, k1, p1, k1] 5 times, k5; rep from *; end last rep k3.

Row 61: *K3, p1, k1, p1, [k5, p1, k1, p1] 5 times; rep from *, end k3.

Row 62: *K3, yo, k1, p1, k1, [p5, k1, p1, k1] 5 times, yo; rep from *, end k3—195 sts.

Row 63: K4, *p1, k1, p1, [k5, p1, k1, p1] 5 times, k5; rep from *, end last rep k4.

Row 64: *K3, [p1, k1] 2 times, [p5, k1, p1, k1] 5 times, p1; rep from *, end k3.

Row 65: K4, *[p1, yo, (k1, p1, k1) in next st, yo, p1, p5tog] 5 times, p1, yo, (k1, p1, k1) in next st, yo, p1, k5; rep from *, end last rep k4—211 sts.

Row 66: *K3, yo, p1, k1, [p5, k1, p1, k1] 5 times, p5, k1, p1, yo; rep from *, end k3—219 sts.

Row 67: *K3, p1, k1, p1, [k5, p1, k1, p1] 6 times; rep from *, end k3.

Row 68: *K4, p1, k1, [p5, k1, p1, k1] 6 times; rep from *, end last rep k3.

Row 69: *K3, p1, k1, p1, [k5, p1, k1, p1] 6 times; rep from *, end k3.

Row 70: *K3, yo, k1 p1, k1, [p5, k1, p1, k1] 6 times, yo; rep from *, end k3—227 sts.

Row 71: K4, *[p1, yo, (k1, p1, k1) in next st, yo, p1, p5tog] 6 times, p1, yo, (k1, p1, k1) in next st, yo,

p1, k5; rep from *, end last rep k4—235 sts.

Row 72: *K3, p1, k1, [p5, k1, p1, k1] 6 times, p5, k1, p1; rep from *, end k3—243 sts.

Row 73: K4, *p1, [k5, p1, k1, p1] 6 times, k5, p1, k5; rep from *, end last rep k4.

Row 74: *K3, yo, p1, k1, [p5, k1, p1, k1] 6 times, p5, k1, p1, yo; rep from *, end k3—251 sts.

Row 75: *K3, p1, k1, p1, [k5, p1, k1, p1] 7 times; rep from *, end k3.

Row 76: *K3, [k1, p1, k1, p5] 7 times, k1, p1, k1; rep from *, end k3.

Row 77: *K3, [p1, yo, (k1, p1, k1) in next st, yo, p1, p5tog] 7 times, p1, yo, (k1, p1, k1) in next st, yo, p1; rep from *, end k3—267 sts.

Row 78: *K3, yo, k1, [p5, k1, p1, k1] 7 times, p5, k1, yo; rep from *, end k3—275 sts.

Row 79: K4, *p1, [k5, p1, k1, p1] 7 times, k5, p1, k5; rep from *, end last rep k4.

Row 80: *K3, p1, k1, [p5, k1, p1, k1] 7 times, p5, k1, p1; rep from *, end k3.

Row 81: K4, *p1, [k5, p1, k1, p1] 7 times, k5, p1, k5; rep from *, end last rep k4.

Row 82: *K3, yo, p1, k1, [p5, k1, p1, k1] 7 times, p5, k1, p1, yo; rep from *, end k3—283 sts.

Row 83: *K3, p1, k1, p1, [p5tog, p1, yo, (k1, p1, k1) in next st, yo, p1] 7 times, p5tog, p1, k1, p1; rep from *, end k3—267 sts.

Row 84: K4, *p1, [k1, p1, k1, p5] 7 times, [k1, p1] 2 times, k5; rep from *, end last rep k4.

Row 85: *K3, p1, k1, [p1, k1, p1, k5] 7 times, [p1, k1] 2 times, p1; rep from *, end k3.

Row 86: *K3, yo, k1, p1, [k1, p1, k1, p5] 7 times, [k1, p1] 2 times, k1, yo; rep from *, end k3—275 sts.

Row 87: *K3, p2, k1, [p1, k1, p1, k5] 7 times, [p1, k1] 2 times, p2; rep from *, end k3.

Row 88: K5, *p1, [k1, p1, k1, p5] 7 times, [k1, p1] 2 times, k7; rep from *, end last rep k5.

Row 89: K4, *p1, k1, [p1, yo, (k1, p1, k1) in next st, yo, p1, p5tog] 7 times, p1, yo, (k1, p1, k1) in next st, yo, p1, k1, p1, k5; rep from *, end last rep k4—291 sts.

Row 90: *K3, yo, p1, [k1, p1, k1, p5] 8 times, [k1, p1] 2 times, yo; rep from *, end k3—299 sts.

Row 91: K5, *[p1, k1, p1, k5] 8 times, p1, k1, p1, k7; rep from *, end last rep k5.

Row 92: *K3, p2, [k1, p1, k1, p5] 8 times, k1, p1, k1, p2; rep from *, end k3.

Row 93: K5, *[p1, k1, p1, k5] times, p1, k1, p1, k7; rep from *, end last rep k5.

Row 94: *K3, yo, p2, [k1, p1, k1, p5] 8 times, k1, p1, k1, p2, yo; rep from *, end k3—307 sts.

Row 95: K6, [p1, yo, (k1, p1, k1) in next st, yo, p1, p5tog] 8 times, p1, yo, (k1, p1, k1) in next st, yo, p1, k9; rep from *, end last rep k6—323 sts.

Row 96: *K3, p1, [k1, p1, k1, p5] 9 times, [k1, p1] 2 times; rep from *, end k3.

Row 97: K4, *[p1, k1, p1, k5] 9 times, p1, k1, p1, k5; rep from *, end last rep k4.

Row 98: *K3, yo, p1, [k1, p1, k1, p5] 9 times, [k1, p1] 2 times, yo; rep from *, end k3—331 sts.

Row 99: K5, *[p1, k1, p1, k5] 9 times, p1, k1, p1, k7; rep from *, end last rep k5.

Row 100: *K3, p2, [k1, p1, k1, p5] 9 times, k1, p1, k1, p2; rep from *, end k3.

Row 101: K5, *[p1, yo, (k1, p1, k1) in next st, yo, p1, p5tog] 9 times, p1, yo, (k1, p1, k1) in next st, yo, p1, k7; rep from *, end last rep k5—347 sts.

Row 102: *K3, yo, [k1, p1, k1, p5] 10 times, k1, p1, k1, yo; rep from *, end k3—355 sts.

Row 103: K4, *[p1, k1, p1, k5] 10 times, p1, k1, p1, k5; rep from *, end last rep k4.

Row 104: *K3, p1, [k1, p1, k1, p5] 10 times, [k1, p1] 2 times; rep from *, end k3.

Row 105: K4, *[p1, k1, p1, k5) 10 times, p1, k1, p1, k5; rep from *, end last rep k4.

Row 106: *K3, yo, p1, [k1, p1, k1, p5] 10 times, [k1, p1] 2 times, yo; rep from *, end k3—363 sts.

Row 107: K5, *[p1, yo, (k1, p1, k1) in next st, yo, p1, p5tog] 10 times, p1, yo, (k1, p1, k1) in next st, yo, p1, k7; rep from *, end last rep k5—379 sts.

Row 108: *K4, p1, k1, [p5, k1, p1, k1] 11 times; rep from *, end k3.

Row 109: *K3, [p1, k1, p1, k5] 11 times, p1, k1, p1; rep from *, end k3.

Row 110: *K3, yo, [k1, p1, k1, p5] 11 times, k1, p1, k1, yo; rep from *, end k3—387 sts.

Row 111: K4, *[p1, k1, p1, k5] 11 times, p1, k1, p1, k5; rep from *, end last rep k4.

Row 112: *K3, p1, [k1, p1, k1, p5] 11 times, [k1, p1] 2 times; rep from *, end k3.

Row 113: K4, *[p1, yo, (k1, p1, k1) in next st, yo, p1, p5tog] 11 times, p1, yo, (k1, p1, k1) in next st, yo, p1, k5; rep from *, end last rep k4—403 sts.

Row 114: *K3, yo, p1, k1, [p5, k1, p1, k1] 11 times, p5, k1, p1, yo; rep from *, end k3—411 sts.

Row 115: *k3, [p1, k1, p1, k5] 12 times, p1, k1, p1; rep from *, end k3.

Row 116: *k4, p1, k1, [p5, k1, p1, k1] 12 times; rep from *, end k3.

Row 117: *K3, [p1, k1, p1, k5] 12 times, p1, k1, p1; rep from *, end k3.

Row 118: *K3, yo, [k1, p1, k1, p5] 12 times, k1, p1, k1, yo; rep from *, end k3—419 sts.

Row 119: K4, *[p1, yo, (k1, p1, k1) in next st, yo, p1, p5tog] 12 times, p1, yo, (k1, p1, k1) in next st, yo, p1, k5; rep from *, end last rep k4—435 sts.

Rows 120–124: *Knit.*

Bind off sts loosely, with as much elasticity as in the knitted fabric. To help do this, yarn over every 3 to 5 sts, and bind off each yo as if it were a st. This adds extra elasticity to the shawl's edge, and is virtually undetectable. Weave in loose ends. Block, making sure that each garter-stitch band is stretched to the same length.

CAT'S PAW SQUARE SHAWL
With two narrow colorbands

This is a rather lacy shawl with Cat's Paw (narrow version) in the center and Old Shale around the outer edge. It features visible yarn-over increases to shape the four corners, and a simple crocheted-off finish. Omit the color bands for a single-color shawl. For best results, use a yarn that can be blocked.

The shawl pictured measures about 52" (132 cm) square. It has a blocked gauge of about 3 stitches and 6 rows per inch, and used 10 ounces of wool singles in the main color and less than 1 ounce of the contrasting color.

Cast on 8 sts and divide evenly among 4 dpn—2 sts each needle. With a 5th dpn, join, being careful not to twist sts. Knit 1 rnd. (Note: Change to cir needle when necessary.)

Rnd 1: *K1, CO 1 st; rep from *— 16 sts.

Rnd 2 and all even-numbered rnds: Knit.

Rnd 3: *K1, yo, k2, yo, k1; rep from *—24 sts.

Rnd 5: *K1, yo, k4, yo, k1; rep from *—32 sts.

Rnd 7: *K1, yo, k6, yo, k1; rep from *—40 sts.

Rnd 9: (Begin Cat's Paw pattern) *[K1, yo] 2 times, ssk, k2, k2tog, [yo, k1] 2 times; rep from *—48 sts.

Rnd 11: *K1, yo, k3, yo, ssk, k2tog, yo, k3, yo, k1; rep from *—56 sts.

Rnd 13: *[K1, yo] 2 times, k3tog, yo, k4, yo, k3tog, [yo, k1] 2 times; rep from *—64 sts.

Rnd 15: *K1, yo, [k1, k2tog, yo, k1, yo, ssk, k1] 2 times, yo, k1; rep from *—72 sts.

KERRY BLUE SQUARE SHAWL
Knitted in the round

This shawl combines three stitch patterns: Feather, Van Dyke and Rib, and Shell. None of these patterns is particularly difficult to knit so don't feel daunted. Because it is worked from the center outward, you can knit it in the gauge and yarn of your choice until it is the size you want. The stitches can accommodate even non-blockable synthetic yarns, if worked in a fairly large, loose gauge of less than four stitches to the inch.

The shawl pictured was made from 16 ounces of blue-gray wool singles and has a blocked measurement of 60" (152.5 cm) square. This shawl is more than ten years old, nicely mended in spots, and well traveled. It has been back and forth across the Atlantic at least three times, and across North America from New York City to San Diego, and from Banff, Alberta, to Mobile Bay, Alabama. If ever there was a "practically perfect" wool shawl, the Kerry Blue is it.

Cast on 3 sts on each of 4 dpn—12 sts. With a 5th needle, join being careful not to twist sts. Knit 1 rnd.

Rnd 1: *K1, [yo, k1] 2 times; rep from *—20 sts.

Rnd 2 and all even rnds unless otherwise noted: Knit.

Rnd 3: *K1, yo, k3, yo, k1; rep from *—28 sts.

Rnd 5: *K1, yo, k5, yo, k1; rep from *—36 sts.

Rnd 7: *K1, yo, k7, yo, k1; rep from *—44 sts

Rnd 9: *K1, yo, k9, yo, k1; rep from *—52 sts.

Rnd 11: *K1, yo, k11, yo, k1; rep from *—60 sts.

Rnd 13: *K1, yo, k13, yo, k1; rep from *—68 sts.

Rnd 15: (Begin Feather patt) *K1, yo, [k2tog, yo] 7 times, k1, yo, k1; rep from *—76 sts.

Rnd 17: *K1, yo, k17, yo, k1; rep from *—84 sts.

Rnd 19: *K1, yo, [k2tog, yo] 9 times, k1, yo, k1; rep from *—92 sts.

Rnd 21: *K1, yo, k21, yo, k1; rep from *—100 sts.

Rnd 23: *K1, yo, [p2, p2tog, yo, k1, yo, ssp] 3 times, p2, yo, k1; rep from *—108 sts.

Rnd 25: *K1, yo, k25, yo, k1; rep from *—116 sts.

Rnd 27: *K1, yo, k2, [p2, p2tog, yo, k1, yo, ssp] 3 times, p2, k2, yo, k1; rep from *—124 sts.

Rnd 29: *K1, yo, k29, yo, k1; rep from *—132 sts.

Rnd 31: *K1, yo, k4, [p2, p2tog, yo, k1, yo, ssp] 3 times, p2, k4, yo, k1; rep from *—140 sts.

Rnd 33: *K1, yo, k33, yo, k1; rep from *—148 sts.

Rnd 35: *K1, yo, p1, p2tog, yo, k1, yo, ssp, [p2, p2tog, yo, k1, yo, ssp] 3 times, p2, p2tog, yo, k1, yo, ssp, p1, yo, k1; rep from *—156 sts.

Rnd 37: *K1, yo, k37, yo, k1; rep from *—164 sts.

Rnd 39: *K1, yo, k1, [p2, p2tog, yo, k1, yo, ssp] 5 times, p2, k1, yo, k1; rep from *—172 sts.

Rnd 41: *K1, yo, k41, yo, k1; rep from *—180 sts.

Rnd 43: *K1, yo, k3, [p2, p2tog, yo, k1, yo, ssp] 5 times, p2, k3, yo, k1; rep from *—188 sts.

Rnds 44–51: Knit, working incs on odd-numbered rnds.

Rnd 52: *K1, p53, k1; rep from *—220 sts.

Rnd 53: *K1, yo, k53, yo, k1—228 sts.

Rnd 54: *K1, p55, k1; rep from *.

Rnds 55–60: Knit, working incs on odd-numbered rnds.

Rnd 61: (Begin Van Dyke and Rib patt) *K1, yo, k3, [k3, yo, ssk, k2, k2tog, yo, k1, yo, ssk] 4 times, k3, yo, ssk, k5, yo, k1; rep from *—260 sts.

Rnd 63: *K1, yo, k4, [k1, k2tog, yo, k1, yo, ssk] 9 times, k5, yo, k1; rep from *—268 sts.

Rnd 65: *K1, yo, [k2tog, yo, k1, yo, ssk, k2tog, yo, k3, yo, ssk] 5 times, k2tog, yo, k1, yo, ssk, yo, k1; rep from *—276 sts.

Rnd 67: *K1, yo, k1, [k2tog, yo, k1, yo, ssk, k3, yo, ssk, k2] 5 times, k2tog, yo, k1, yo, ssk, k1, yo, k1; rep from *—284 sts.

Rnd 69: *K1, yo, k2, [k2tog, yo, k1, yo, ssk, k1] 11 times, k1, yo, k1; rep from *—292 sts.

Rnd 71: *K1, yo, k3, [k2tog, yo, k1, yo, ssk, k2tog, yo, k3, yo, ssk] 5 times, k2tog, yo, k1, yo, ssk, k3, yo, k1; rep from *—300 sts.

Rnd 73: *K1, yo, k4, [k2tog, yo, k1, yo, ssk, k3, yo, ssk, k2] 5 times, k2tog, yo, k1, yo, ssk, k4, yo, k1; rep from *—308 sts.

Rnd 75: *K1, yo, k5, [k2tog, yo, k1, yo, ssk, k1] 11 times, k4, yo, k1; rep from *—316 sts.

Rnd 77: *K1, yo, k6, [k2tog, yo, k1, yo, ssk, k2tog, yo, k3, yo, ssk] 5 times, k2tog, yo, k1, yo, ssk, k6, yo, k1; rep from *—324 sts.

Rnd 79: *K1, yo, k3, yo, ssk, k2, [k2tog, yo, k1, yo, ssk, k3, yo, ssk, k2] 5 times, k2tog, yo, k1, yo, ssk, k3, yo, ssk, k2, yo, k1; rep from *—332 sts.

Rnd 81: *K1, yo, k2, [k2tog, yo, k1, yo, ssk, k1] 13 times, k1, yo, k1; rep from *—340 sts.

Rnd 83: *K1, yo, k2, [k2tog, yo, k3, yo, ssk, k2tog, yo, k1, yo, ssk] 6 times, k2tog, yo, k3, yo, ssk, k2, yo, k1; rep from *—348 sts.

Rnd 85: *K1, yo, k3, [k3, yo, ssk, k2, k2tog, yo, k1, yo, ssk] 6 times, k3, yo, ssk, k5, yo, k1; rep from *—356 sts.

Rnd 87: *K1, yo, k5, [k2tog, yo, k1, yo, ssk, k1] 13 times, k4, yo, k1; rep from *—364 sts.

Rnd 89: *K1, yo, [k2tog, yo, k1, yo, ssk, k2tog, yo, k3, yo, ssk] 7 times, k2tog, yo, k1, yo, ssk, yo, k1; rep from *—372 sts.

Rnds 90–93: Knit, working incs on odd-numbered rnds.

Rnd 94: *K1, p95, k1; rep from *—388 sts

Rnd 95: *K1, yo, k95, yo, k1; rep from *—396 sts.

Rnd 96: *K1, p97, k1; rep from *.

Rnds 97–100: Knit, working incs on odd-numbered rnds.

Rnd 101: (Begin Shell patt) *K1, yo, k1, [p2tog twice, yo, (k1, yo) 3 times, p2tog twice] 9 times, k1, yo, k1; rep from *—420 sts.

Rnd 103: *K1, yo, k103, yo, k1; rep from *—428 sts.

Rnd 105: *K1, yo, k3, [p2tog twice, yo, (k1, yo) 3 times, p2tog twice] 9 times, k3, yo, k1; rep from *—436 sts.

Rnd 107: *K1, yo, k107, yo, k1; rep from *—444 sts.

Rnd 109: *K1, yo, k2, yo, k1, p2tog, [p2tog twice, yo, (k1, yo) 3 times, p2tog twice] 9 times, p2tog, k1, yo, k2, yo, k1; rep from *—452 sts.

Rnd 111: *K1, yo, k111, yo, k1; rep from *—460 sts.

Rnd 113: *K1, yo, k2, yo, k1, yo, p2tog twice, [p2tog twice, yo, (k1, yo) 3 times, p2tog twice] 9 times, p2tog twice, yo, k1, yo, k2, yo, k1; rep from *—468 sts.

Rnd 115: *K1, yo, k115, yo, k1; rep from *—476 sts.

Rnd 117: *K1, yo, k1, p2tog, yo, [k1, yo] 2 times, p2tog twice, [p2tog twice, yo, (k1, yo) 3 times) p2tog twice] 9 times, p2tog twice, [yo, k1] 2 times, yo, p2tog, k1, yo, k1; rep from *—484 sts.

Rnd 119: *K1, yo, k119, yo, k1; rep from *—492 sts.

Rnd 121: *K1, yo, [p2tog twice, yo, (k1, yo) 3 times, p2tog twice] 11 times, yo k1; rep from *—500 sts.

Rnd 123: *K1, yo, k123, yo, k1; rep from *—508 sts.

Rnd 125: *K1, yo, k2, [p2tog twice, yo, (k1, yo) 3 times, p2tog twice] 11 times, k2, yo, k1; rep from *—516 sts.

Rnd 127: *K1, yo, k127, yo, k1; rep from *—524 sts.

Rnd 129: *K1, [yo, k1] 2 times, p2tog, [p2tog twice, yo, (k1, yo) 3 times, p2tog twice] 11 times, p2tog, [k1, yo] 2 times, k1; rep from *—532 sts.

Rnd 131: *K1, yo, k131, yo, k1; rep from *—540 sts.

Rnd 133: *[K1, yo] 3 times, p2tog twice, [p2tog twice, yo, (k1, yo) 3 times, p2tog twice] 11 times, p2tog twice, [yo, k1] 3 times; rep from *—548 sts.

Rnd 135: *K1, yo, k135, yo, k1; rep from *—556 sts.

Rnd 137: *K1, yo, p2tog, yo, [k1, yo] 2 times, p2tog twice, [p2tog twice, yo, (k1, yo) 3 times, p2tog twice] 11 times, p2tog twice, [yo, k1] 2 times, yo, p2tog, yo, k1; rep from *—564 sts.

Rnds 138–145: Knit, working incs on odd-numbered rnds.

Rnd 139: *K1, yo, k139, yo, k1; rep from *—572 sts.

Rnd 141: *K1, yo, k2, [k1, yo] 2 times, p2tog twice, [p2tog twice, yo, (k1, yo) 3 times, p2tog twice] 11 times, p2tog twice, [yo, k1] 2 times, k2, yo, k1; rep from *—580 sts.

Rnd 146: *K1, p147, k1; rep from *—596 sts.

Rnd 147: *K1, yo, k147, yo, k1; rep from *—604 sts.

Rnd 148: *K1, p149, k1; rep from *.

Rnds 149–154: Knit, working incs on odd-numbered rnds.

Rnd 155: (Begin outer border) *[K1, yo] 2 times, k2tog, yo, [k4, (yo, k2tog) 2 times] 19 times, yo, k1; rep from *—640 sts.

Rnd 157: *K1, yo, k1, [k2tog, yo] 2 times, [k4, (yo, k2tog) 2 times] 19 times, k1, yo, k1; rep from *—648 sts.

Rnd 159: *K1, yo, k2tog, yo, k4, [(yo, k2tog) 2 times, k4] 19 times, yo, k2tog, yo, k1; rep from *—656 sts.

Rnd 161: *K1, yo, k1, k2tog, yo, k4, [(yo, k2tog) 2 times, k4] 19 times, yo, k2tog, k1, yo, k1; rep from *—664 sts.

Rnd 163: *K1, yo, [k4, (yo, k2tog) 2 times] 20 times, k4, yo, k1; rep from *—672 sts.

Rnd 165: *K1, yo, k1, [k4, (yo, k2tog) 2 times], 20 times, k5, yo, k1; rep from *—680 sts.

Rnd 167: *K1, yo, k168, yo, k1; rep from *—688 sts.

Rnd 169: *K1, yo, k170, yo, k1; rep from *—696 sts.

Rnd 170: With crochet hook, *ch 3tog, ch 5; rep from *. Cut yarn and draw end through last loop.

Finishing: Weave in loose ends. Block.

CHILDREN OF LIR RECTANGLE STOLE

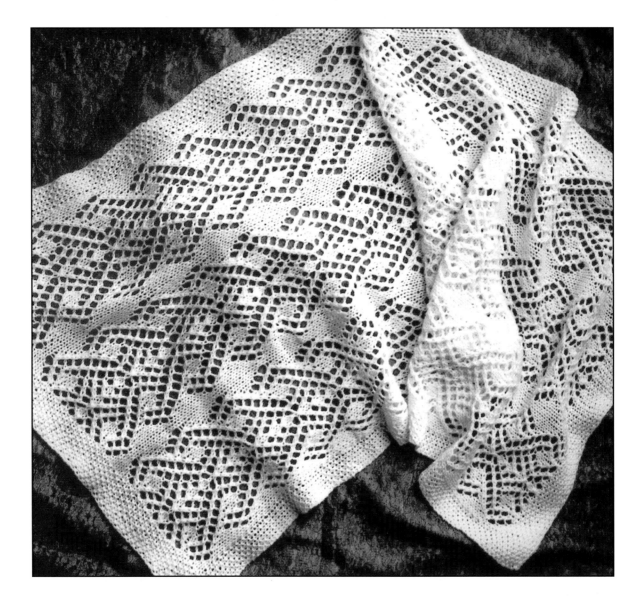

This evening stole is inspired by an ancient Irish tale about the children of a king named Lir (pronounced Leer) who are turned into swans by their jealous step-mother ("The Fate of the Children of Lir" in *More Celtic Fairytales* by Joseph Jacob; Dover Publications, 1968). The lace pattern, called "Wings of the Swan", is repeated three times across the width, and is bordered on all four sides with seed stitch. The stole is worked from provisionally cast-on stitches at the center back outward to each side so that the "wings" are centered when the stole is worn.

The stole pictured was made with 6½ ounces of two-ply sport-weight wool on size 10 (6 mm) needles. It has a blocked measurement of 24" (61 cm) wide by 60" (152 cm) long.

Stitches

Double Decrease (dbl dec): *Sl 2 tog as to knit, k1, p2sso.*

Seed stitch:

Row 1: *K1, p1; rep from *.*
Row 2: Knit the purls and purl the knits.
Rep Row 2 for pattern.

Using the provisional method (see page 108), cast on 83 sts. Break off waste yarn.

Row 1: Work 7 sts in Seed st, [k4, (k2tog, yo) 2 times, k1, yo, ssk, k1, k2tog, yo, k1, (yo, ssk) 2 times, k4] 3 times, work 7 sts in Seed st.

Row 2 and all WS rows: Work 7 sts in Seed st, p69, work 7 sts in Seed st.

Row 3: Work 7 sts in Seed st, [k3, (k2tog, yo) 2 times, k1, yo, ssk, yo, dbl dec, yo, k2tog, yo, k1, (yo, ssk) 2 times, k3] 3 times, work 7 sts in Seed st.

Row 5: Work 7 sts in Seed st, [k2, (k2tog, yo)2 times, k1, (yo, ssk)

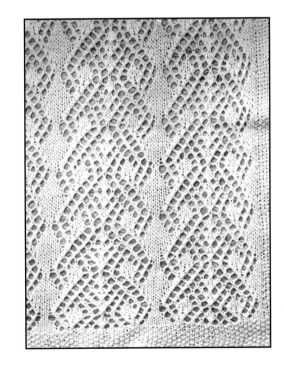

2 times, k1, (k2tog, yo) 2 times, k1, (yo, ssk) 2 times, k2] 3 times, work 7 sts in Seed st.

Row 7: Work 7 sts in Seed st, [k1, (k2tog, yo) 2 times, k3, yo, ssk, yo, dbl dec, yo, k2tog, yo, k3, (yo, ssk) 2 times, k1] 3 times, work 7 sts in Seed st.

Row 9: Work 7 sts in Seed st, [k1, (yo, ssk) 2 times, k2, (k2tog, yo) 2 times, k1, (yo, ssk) 2 times, k2 (k2tog, yo) 2 times, k1] 3 times, work 7 sts in Seed st.

Row 11: Work 7 sts in Seed st,

[k2, (yo, ssk) 2 times, (k2tog, yo) 2 times, k3, (yo, ssk) 2 times, (k2tog, yo) 2 times, k2] 3 times, work 7 sts in Seed st.

Row 13: Work 7 sts in Seed st, [k3, yo, ssk, (k2tog, yo) 2 times, k1, yo, dbl dec, yo, k1, (yo, ssk) 2 times, k2tog, yo, k3] 3 times, work 7 sts in Seed st.

Row 14: Rep Row 2.

Rep Rows 1–14 eight more times.

Work 12 rows of Seed st across all sts for border. Bind off all sts

loosely. Carefully remove the waste yarn from the cast-on row and place the sts on a needle. Rep from Row 1 for the other half of the stole.

Finishing: Weave in loose ends. Block to a consistent width, using lots of pins along the Seed st borders to keep them straight. If the borders look scalloped, add more pins along the edges and/or slacken the tension slightly. Leave pins in until stole is completely dried.

PROVISIONAL CAST-ON

This provisional cast-on uses the continental method with a main yarn and a waste yarn.

Leaving tails about 4" long, tie a length of waste yarn together with the main yarn in an overhand knot. With your right hand, hold the knot on top of the needle a short distance from the tip, then place your thumb and index finger between the two yarns and hold the long ends with your other fingers. Hold your hand with your palm facing upwards and spread your thumb and finger apart so that the yarn forms a V with the main yarn over your index finger and the waste yarn over your thumb. Bring the needle up through the waste-yarn loop on your thumb from front to back. Place the needle over the main yarn on your finger, and then back through the loop on your thumb. Drop the loop off your thumb and, placing your thumb back in the V configuration, tighten up the stitch

on the needle. Repeat for the desired number of stitches. The main yarn will form the stitches on the needle and the waste yarn will make the horizontal ridge at the base of the cast-on row.

When it is time to pick up the cast-on stitches for working them in the opposite direction, carefully pull out the waste yarn as you place the exposed loops on a needle. Take care to pick up the loops so that they are in the proper orientation before you begin knitting.

Garter Lace Triangle Shawl

This shawl is simple to make. Six rows of garter stitch alternate with four rows of lace in bands that are about the same width. You can widen either band by 2, 4, or 6 rows, if desired. You can make the shawl more lacy with more lace rows, or more sturdy with more garter-stitch rows. Its simplicity makes this shawl suitable for nearly any yarn, from slubby cotton to wool lace-weight or singles to acrylic/wool blends.

The shawl pictured was worked with 4 ½ ounces of 4-ply fingering weight wool/nylon blend (75% wool, 25% nylon) on size 5 (3.75 mm) needles. It measures 58" (147.5 cm) from tip to tip and 28" (71 cm) long.

Note: Increases are made in the first and last stitch of every right-side row. To help keep track of increase rows, attach a safety pin to the right side of the piece after you have worked a few rows.

Cast on 4 sts. Knit 1 row.

Rows 1, 3, and 5: (RS) K1 f&b, knit to last st, k1 f&b—2 sts inc'd.

Rows 2, 4, and 6: Knit.

Rows 7 and 9: K1 f&b, k1, *yo, k2tog; rep from * to last 2 sts, k1, k1 f&b—2 sts inc'd.

Rows 8 and 10: K3, *yo, p2tog; rep from * to last 3 sts, k3.

Rep Rows 1–10 to desired length, ending with Row 6. Bind off all sts loosely to maintain elasticity. Alternatively, you can finish the piece with a narrow knitted-on border.

Finishing: Weave in loose ends. Block.

Abbreviations

BO Bind off.

CO Cast on.

dec Decrease (subtract one or two stitches, as specified).

dbl dec Double decrease—Decrease two stitches: Sl 2 tog knitwise, k1, p2sso.

dpn Double-pointed needle.

inc Increase (add one or more stitches, as specified).

k Knit.

k1 f&b Knit through the front loop, and then through the back loop of a stitch (increases one stitch).

M1 Make 1—Pick up the horizontal bar that lies between two stitches on the needles (increases one stitch).

p Purl.

psso Pass slipped stitch (on right needle) over next stitch, as if binding it off.

RS Right side.

sl Slip—Pass a stitch from the left needle to the right needle without knitting it. Unless otherwise instructed, always slip a stitch as if you were purling it (sl purlwise).

ssk Slip, slip, knit—Slip two stitches knitwise (one at a time) onto right needle, then insert tip of left needle into the front of these two stitches, and knit them together through the back loops with the right needle.

ssp Slip, slip, purl—Slip two stitches knitwise (one at a time) onto right needle, then insert tip of left needle into the front of these two stitches, and purl them together through the back loops with the right needle.

st(s) Stitch(es).

tbl Through back loop—Work the stitch through the loop on the back side of the needle, not the loop on the front side, as is usual.

tog Together.

WS Wrong side.

yo Yarn over—Pass the yarn over the top of the right needle before working the next stitch—an increase method that leaves a hole in the fabric, used for lace stitches.

Chart Symbols

□	k on RS; p on WS	∟	k in front and back of st
•	p on RS; k on WS	⌐	p in front and back of st
O	yo	V	sl 1 with yarn in back on RS
③	yo specified number of times	ⴸ	sl 1 with yarn in back on WS
/	k2tog on RS; p2tog on WS	ⴸ③	k1, p1, k1 in same st
\	ssk on RS; ssp on WS	ⴸ4	k4tog
⟍	p2tog tbl	ⴸ	k4tog tbl
⟋	p2tog	⌃5	purl specified number of sts tog
M	make 1	⌃15	p15tog
b	k1 tbl on RS; p1 tbl on WS	▨	no stitch
⋀	dbl dec: sl 2tog as to knit, k1, p2sso	⧄	sl 1, k2, psso or sl 1, k3, psso
⟋	k3tog on RS, p3tog on WS	⌒	bind off
⟍	p3tog on RS, k3tog on WS	⑥	(p1, k1) 3 times in same st

111

APPENDIX

NUMBER OF STITCHES NEEDED TO FIT AROUND CIRCULAR NEEDLES				
Your gauge in stitches per inch	**Length of circular needle**			
	16"	24"	29"	36"
3	48	72	90	120
3.5	56	84	105	135
4	64	96	120	150
4.5	72	108	135	165
5	80	120	150	180
5.5	88	132	165	195
6	96	144	180	216
6.5	104	156	195	234
7	112	168	210	252
7.5	120	180	225	270
8	128	192	240	288
8.5	136	204	255	306
9	144	216	270	324

If you have begun knitting a round or square shawl on double-pointed needles, at a gauge of 4 stitches per inch, you can transfer your knitting to a 16" circular needle when you have reached 64 stitches, and a 24" needle when you have reached 96 stitches. This chart also can help you determine what size circular needle to use for other circular knitting, such as sweaters, ponchos, or skirts.

OTHER OPTIONS FOR SHAWL BLOCKING

Cork or dense-foam wallboard. Either cork or the dense foam used for insulation may be mounted on a wall and used to block shawls. Cork may be used uncovered, but the foam looks best if painted or covered with fabric. The disadvantage to this method is that you must hold up the damp shawl as you spread out and pin it to the cork or foam. It's easier to manage if you have a helper. The advantage to this method is that the shawl is out of the way as it dries. To help you pin your shawl out evenly, draw circles, rectangles, or squares on the board with pencil or indelible ink.

Stretcher frame. You can make a stretcher frame out of four lengths of 1"-by-2" boards, four 2"- to 4"-wide strips of tightly woven fabric, and four C-clamps. Cut the boards 12" longer than you expect the sides of the shawl to stretch to. Cut the fabric strips a few inches shorter than the lengths of the boards and staple one (centered) to each board. Clearly mark the midpoint of each board and fabric strip. Pin the midpoint of one side of the shawl to the mark on the fabric strip, then pin the shawl edges to the fabric, stretching gently, both directions to the corners. Repeat for each side of the shawl. Where the corners of the boards overlap, clamp them together with C-clamps, stretching the boards apart as you clamp—brace one board against your leg while you push the other board outward, have the clamp in position, and tighten it down when that corner is taut. You can set the frame upright until the shawl has dried. Then loosen the clamps and remove the pins.

The old Scottish stretcher frames were similar but had wooden or metal pegs along each board and holes in each corner to take the place of clamps. Some knitters liked to run a cotton thread through each point in a scarf's edging and loop the thread over the pegs of the stretcher. This prevented the shawl from touching the frame.

Pinning out on the lawn. Though not recommend this for your best work and rather crude, you can block your shawls on the lawn with a few tent stakes, mallet, clothesline rope, measuring tape, and plenty of spring clothespins. Measuring as you go, hammer the stakes into the ground in the shape of your shawl, but in a slightly larger circumference than you expect the finished shawl to be: three stakes for a triangle, four for a square or rectangle, five for a half circle, and eight for a circle. Then tie the clothesline to one stake and stretch it around the circumference of the remaining stakes, wrapping it once around each stake as you go. Tie the clothesline again to the first stake. You will have an outline of your shawl shape. If you'd like, spread a sheet on the ground inside this outline. Next, spread your shawl on the ground (or sheet) and use the clothespins to clip the edges of the shawl to the clothesline. You may have to adjust the stakes slightly as you go. Begin pinning the corners, then the center of each edge, then pin along all the remaining edges. Your shawl will sag in the middle, but that's okay. To protect against sun, birds, tree sap, or other outdoor hazards, cover the shawl with another sheet until it is dry. If it begins to rain, you can pull up the tent stakes and whisk the whole thing indoors.

BIBLIOGRAPHY

Ames, Frank. "Guide to Paisley Shawls" in *The Paisley Pattern*. Layton, Utah: Gibbs Smith, Publisher, 1987.

Bennett, Helen. *Scottish Knitting*. Alyesbury: Shire Publications, 1986.

Blair, Matthew. *The Paisley Shawl and the Men Who Produced It*. Paisley: Alexander Gardener, 1904.

Burnham, Dorothy. *Cut My Cote*. Toronto: The Royal Ontario Museum, 1973.

Carroll, Amy, ed. *Traditional Knitting*. The Pattern Library Series, New York: Ballantine Books, 1983.

Carter Scott, Barbara. "The Shetlands' Fine Tradition." *Spin-Off* (Winter 1989), 58–66.

Clabburn, Pamela. *Shawls*. Aylesbury: Shire Publications, 1981.

Compton, Rae. *The Complete Book of Traditional Knitting*. London: B. T. Batsford, Ltd., 1983.

Don, Sarah. *The Art of Shetland Lace*. London: Bell and Hyman, Ltd., 1981; San Francisco: Lacis, 1992.

Goldthorpe, Caroline. *From Queen to Empress; Victorian Dress 1837–1877*. New York: The Metropolitan Museum of Art, 1988.

Harvey, Michael and Rae Compton. *Fisherman Knitting*. Aylesbury: Shire Publications, 1978.

Macdonald, Anne L. *No Idle Hands: The Social History of American Knitting*. New York: Ballantine Books, 1988.

McGregor, Sheila. *Traditional Knitting*. London: B. T. Batsford, Ltd., 1983.

Mills, Betty J. *Calico Chronicle*. Lubbock: Texas Technical University Press, 1985.

Mon Tricot Knitting Dictionary. Paris: Mon Tricot Monthly, 1981.

Norbury, James. *Traditional Knitting Patterns*. New York: Dover Publications, 1973.

Reilly, Valerie. *The Paisley Pattern*. Layton, Utah: Gibbs Smith, Publisher, 1987.

Rossbach, Ed. *The Art of Paisley*. New York: Van Nostrand Reinhold Company, 1980.

Rutt, Richard, Bishop of Leicester. *A History of Handknitting*. Loveland, Colorado: Interweave Press, 1987.

——. "The Real Romance of Knitting." *Knitter's* (Winter 1987), 10–13.

Smith, Mary and Chris Bunyan. *A Shetland Knitter's Notebook*. Lerwick, Shetland, Scotland: The Shetland Times, 1991.

Starmore, Alice. "Unravelling the Myths of Shetland Lace." *Threads* (June/July 1989), 41–47.

Strand, Paul and Basil Davidson. *Tir a' Mhurain.* New York: Aperture Books, Grossman Publishers, 1968.

Thomas, Mary. *Mary Thomas's Book of Knitting Patterns.* New York: Dover Publications, 1972.

———. *Mary Thomas's Knitting Book.* New York: Dover Publications, 1972.

Thompson, Gladys. *Patterns for Guernseys, Jerseys and Arans.* New York: Dover Publications, 1971.

Upitis, Lizbeth. "Ah, Shawls." *Knitter's* (Winter 1987), 14–15.

HRH Queen Victoria. *Our Life in the Highlands.* London: William Kimber, 1968.

Walker, Barbara. *A Treasury of Knitting Patterns.* New York: Charles Scribner's Sons, 1968.

Wheeler, Monroe, ed. *Textiles and Ornaments of India.* New York: The Museum of Modern Art, 1956.

Zimmermann, Elizabeth. *Knitter's Almanac.* New York: Charles Scribner's Sons, 1974.

———. *Knitting Workshop.* Pittsville, Wisconsin: Schoolhouse Press, 1981.

INDEX